# Myrtle Fillmore's Healing Letters

UNITY BOOKS
Unity Village, MO 64065

SIXTEENTH PRINTING
August 1986

# In Appreciation

This book is made up of extracts from the letters of Myrtle Page Fillmore, "mother of Unity," as she was lovingly called and as she was in its founding. By her mothering spirit of love and faith and service, in cooperation with her husband Charles Fillmore, she molded Unity and upheld it during the years of its growth.

As the letters from which these extracts were taken blessed and lifted those to whom they were sent, it is hoped that they will do this for others as they now go forth in printed form; that they will bless students everywhere and thus extend Myrtle Fillmore's ministry on this plane, as she is now extending it on that other plane to which she said she was called for another phase of Christ ministry.

*The preparation of these pages for your perusal has been a service of love undertaken in appreciation of a great soul, the mother of Unity. It has been like being again in her presence and receiving instruction and inspiration from the Christ mind that spoke so freely through her; like receiving a benediction from her. May you too, as you read these pages, receive from that Christ to whom she always pointed all who came to her, some of the fire of her inspiration, some of the steadfastness of her faith, some of the zeal she had for Truth, as well as the wisdom and understanding with which she handled all problems, the love she so freely bestowed on all; and may you, as you are lifted, use these Christ attributes as she used them: to inspire your brother and lift the race in its ongoing to glory.*

FRANCES W. FOULKS

# CONTENTS

# My Love to Thee

*Adapted from "The Rosary"*

By Myrtle Fillmore

*The hours I've spent with Thee, dear Lord,*
*Are pearls of priceless worth to me.*
*My soul, my being merge in sweet accord*
*In love for Thee; in love for Thee.*

*Each hour a pearl, each pearl a prayer,*
*Binding Thy presence close to me;*
*I only know that Thou art there, and I*
*Am lost in Thee.*

*Oh, glorious joys that thrill and bless!*
*Oh, visions sweet of love divine!*
*My soul its rapturous bliss can ill express*
*That Thou art mine, O Lord! that Thou art*
*mine.*

*Myrtle Fillmore's Healing Letters*

# Myrtle Fillmore

THE FOLLOWING EXTRACTS FROM HER LETTERS IN-
TRODUCE MYRTLE PAGE FILLMORE TO YOU AS SHE
HERSELF KNEW HERSELF AND AS NO ONE ELSE COULD

YOU see, dear, we just feel rather modest—
really we haven't much to say, as to when
the work was started, and how it was done!
We just received from the Father some ideas
that proved wonderfully helpful in our own
family; and then we shared them with others,
and they too were helped. Since those of like
faith are drawn together, we soon found ourselves in a little society, which was formed for
the study of Truth and the practice of its ideas.
We grew. After a time it seemed that the other
folks went their various ways, and only we were
left to continue what we felt to be important
enough to develop and to devote ourselves to.
And Unity School unfolded and continued to
grow.

We have never cared to interest folks in our
own individual lives. It makes no real difference
to others what we have done, who we are. What
is important is that we are doing what the Father
has given us to do, according to our best light.

13

And if we have something that others want or that will help them—spiritual ideas and their radiance—we are glad to share it. If others wish to receive, all right; if not, because of what they may term our personal limitations, that is all right too. We are not trying to interest folks in the School, but in the ideas of the Christ Mind, which we feel to be the foundation of the work, and our standard of life.

\*    \*    \*

But, dear, I feel you are crowning me with an honor that belongs to the Holy Spirit—which is omnipresent, and which expresses in the loving desires of the hearts of all those who are endeavoring to manifest the Mother side of God! You call me the mother of Unity! Well, now, I know of nothing that would give me greater joy than to feel that God could work so perfectly through me as to bring forth a great ministry and a place of peace and good will and health such as this [Unity School] is; but in reality, I feel that I am only the soul who caught the first vision of this ministry, and who nurtured that vision until others came along to help in the establishment of it in the minds and hearts of our dear ones, and to help in the molding in substance the outer forms of this school and its work.

It is my great joy to perceive somewhat of the Mother side of God—the divine love that never fails and that is equal to the drawing of souls to itself. It is my prayer to be able to radiate the qualities of this divine love to all. You too are the mother of Unity, because in your heart you have the same ideals, and the same great generous spirit, and the endless and tireless service, and the love that never fails! The Mother of Unity is the universal Mother. How happy we are, to represent this Mother!

\*     \*     \*

You may never have suspected it, but this Unity work is a dream that has been nurtured and built from the invisible to the concrete through love and devotion and good, hard work. It may never have occurred to you that my husband and I have put ourselves into this thing which God has given us to do, year after year, without personal returns beyond our "daily bread" and clothing. I work here in the Unity buildings every day, and receive a salary, just as several hundred other workers do. I think a very capable business man or woman would not consider working for that salary. But it meets my personal needs; and usually I have a little each week with which to do what my heart prompts.

*       *       *

We are helping all who come our way to unite with us in the study of the Truth that enables each one to bring forth sufficient supply for daily needs, and to make good use of all the riches of God here in the earth as well as in the heavens of mind.

I am glad to offer you the testimony that we have proved that God can and will prosper the work that the Holy Spirit prompts. As the needs of other branches of our work have arisen, we have let them be known, and the supply and the necessary help with the ministry have come forth. But we have always had to launch right out on faith without visible evidence of the ultimate success. We know that God is in His work, and that it is the Spirit of God operative in a given service that provides whatever is required in the doing of that work.

*       *       *

I myself was once an emaciated little woman, upon whom relatives and doctors had placed the stamp "T.B." [tuberculosis]. And this was only one of the ailments—there were others considered beyond any help, except possibly the changing of structures through an operation. There were family problems too. We were a sickly lot, and came to the place where we were unable to provide for our children. In the midst of all this gloom, we kept looking for the way out, which we felt sure would be revealed. It was! The light of God revealed to us—the thought came to me first—that life was of God, that we were inseparably one with the source, and that we inherited from the divine and per̄fect Father. What that revelation did to me at first was not apparent to the senses. But it held my mind up above the negation, and I began to claim my birthright and to act as though I believed myself the child of God, filled with His life. I gained. And others saw that there was something new in me. And they asked me to share it. I did. Others were healed, and began to study. My husband continued his business, and at first took little interest in what I was doing. But after a time he became absorbed in the study of Truth too. Then we consecrated ourselves to the Lord, and kept doing daily that which we felt led to do. We began to prosper, a little at a time, and our health continued to improve. Life became sweeter and more interesting, and we began to see a new world. In all these years, our interest has not lagged, and we have continued to enjoy the unfoldment of God's plan in our lives.

\*     \*     \*

I'm going to tell you a secret: I don't get to keep house as much as I should like. I'm not supposed to have time for it—folks demand so much of my time. And so I have a woman to keep house for us. But do you know, I like to carry the dishes away from the table at the close of the meal; and then make a nice hot suds and wash the dishes, wipe them, and put them away in nice rows in the china closet! So if sometimes you find yourself doing work that isn't supposed to be desirable, just remember that there are other good folks doing the same sort of work, and that still others would like to be doing it, even though circumstances have placed them at something else. Whatever you undertake, do it the very best you can. And folks will note your good work, and soon you will be given more important positions. Just show the Father that you are ready to do your best, and He will keep increasing your ability and will place you where you will be blessed and where your work will bless others.

\*      \*      \*

I often think these days that we are all in too much of a rush, trying to do too much, and still failing to discern and do the very things that would mean most. So much that we think and do, surely, would not be done by one in the

Jesus Christ consciousness. So much that we think we need would not be desired by one conscious of the spiritual resources.

Indeed, I have felt myself in a strange land and longing for familiar landmarks! And when I feel such a hungering, I try to draw very close to the Father and just rest in the assurance that comes that all is well. I know that He would not have me struggle with unknown things, or talk of that which I have not proved. I realize that that which He would have me do He inspires in me, that it is very easy to do His will, and that when I thus conduct myself a great peace and friendliness comes and abides.

We must have quiet and opportunity for inward searching. For we must go beyond what we have heretofore attained. And there is nothing in hearsay or in observation or in the evidence of the senses, apart from spiritual discernment, that can take us beyond our present footing.

\*     \*     \*

Know this, dear, that I know I must *be* beautiful within, and in my fellowship with others, and in my sharing with them the good things of life *if* I am to become beautiful without. Anything that makes me have the feeling of selfishness cannot result in more beauty to me. Anything that awakens in me the loving desire to have others happy and adorned with beautiful things, and anything that helps me to express this loving desire in my own living is sure to bring forth its fruit in my own life. Now, I am sure that you understand, and approve my passing on to another the use of the beautiful gift that you with so much love sent to me. You did mean for me to use it in the way it would give me most joy, didn't you?

*      *      *

I was very religiously trained and suffered a lot from the terrible theology taught of a God who in truth is *loving*. But I am rejoicing in the doctrine of our wise and loving heavenly Father who chooses that none shall perish but that all shall have eternal life.

Now, one more word: I think you are trying to give me too much credit for your poise and happiness and success! Of course I am happy to have been privileged to write to you and pray with you and rejoice with you over demonstrations. But I know that it is God in the midst of you doing His perfect work who is responsible for the good.

*      *      *

You ask what restored me to vigorous

health. It was a change of mind from the old, carnal mind that believes in sickness to the Christ Mind of life and permanent health. "Be ye transformed by the renewing of your mind." "As he thinketh within himself, so is he." I applied spiritual laws effectively, blessing my body temple until it manifested the innate health of Spirit. These wonderful laws will work for you too when you apply them diligently and in faith.

\* \* \*

I smiled as I read of the state of your finances. I think I'll tell you a little about mine! You know I am on a salary, just as the other Unity folks are. And sometimes I have a very definite place for all my allowance, before I even begin on my own individual needs. Sometimes I am obliged to draw upon the Fillmore account in order to do something I feel to be important. Usually when I find myself "strapped," someone who doesn't know the facts will send me a love gift. Last week I handed out just about all I could get my hands on and was looking for more, because I had places for it. This morning a letter came from a woman to whom I have written a few times, but whom I haven't seen, in which there was a check for *me* for two hundred dollars. No particular apparent reason for her sending it; but evidently she and the Lord were aware of my use of money and replenished my purse in that happy way. So the money I had sent forth came back multiplied; I can replace the amount I drew out and still have plenty of "pin money" left.

\*    \*    \*

I confess that I haven't always looked at man and his work, and his abilities as I now do. There was a time when I felt I must go back to old ways to earn money to meet pressing needs. But my faith and the faith of those who could see a little further along the course that had been indicated than I, helped to hold me steadfast. And I reasoned that my past experiences had not been really satisfying, that I could at least turn my mind to new ideas and give them a thorough trial. I determined to use my ability in the manner that seemed to meet the needs of persons who came my way. I had certain little proofs that I was using a law and that there was substance and life backing me and coming forth at my command.

Now, while it may be that this work in which we are engaged is something that we began in another life—and it doubtless is a science that the universal Christ Mind is pouring forth through us—we do know that the same mind and the same law is in all and operative for all. And that faith and understanding and the determination to live according to the Creator's plan will bring forth whatever is needed, will do just this for everyone who puts his trust fully in the Father.

\* \* \*

From our own experience we find it wise not to talk too much about what we are discovering and using—except to those who really come to us for it. We know that it is not wise or profitable to call attention to differences, not even in the effort to explain our point. If we were to go into other churches or classes, we should endeavor to avoid points of difference or apparent contradictions. We should look for all the points on which to agree, and praise the other's faith and good works. We should talk deliberately on subjects that intuition made us to know the others were interested in. We should not stamp our faith "Unity" or give undue weight to points of doctrine. We should keep to Jesus Christ, the Holy Spirit, as the source of our light and the application of His teaching as the way of life. We should give God the glory for any and all good in our life, and emphasize the Truth that it is His working in and through the individual that does the transforming. We should not, however, be at all disturbed about the prejudice of those who feel that they must show fight and shut out the undesirable. When we began our study and work, we might have had only a handful of friends—if we had thought to look about us and count them. And we no doubt would have met with objections on all sides from the churches if we had given them opportunity to object. But now—well, we just haven't the time to meet and enjoy all the thousands of good friends, hundreds of whom are ministers, who are finding our work safe and our literature food for thought. You will find that if you just love folks and live happily among them, they will love you. If you do not try to change them or give them what they have no knowledge of wanting, they will not show fight or resentment. If you do not in your own attitude or inference show disapproval of their beliefs or ways, they will tear down their walls of opposition and indifference and after a while show an interest in what you have.

No one wants to feel that what he has and has been depending on is false and unreliable. But all want to add to the treasures they now have, and all will in time drop the worthless pebbles for the precious gems—when they have awakened to the point of knowing the difference. So rather than feel that you must "stand up for Truth if it is ridiculed," just let the Truth in you stand for itself. How can a thing be ridiculed, really? If one who knows the Truth and takes not account of evil just keeps poised and loving, that is proof enough. One who speaks an untruth or is mistaken in his judgments has the Christ Mind within him to correct him. You do not need to do this. Leave it with Him. And why compare Unity with other teachings? That is not the Unity way. Unless some earnest soul, God-drawn, comes to you for an explanation or light on some point, better just to let all form their own conclusions. The adverse states of mind are built through some sort of contradition or lack of understanding —and of course they can but contradict that which would set them at naught. Those who don't know Jesus, the real Son of God manifest in the individual, will perhaps contradict the principles embodied. But what of that? The day will come when all adverse states of mind will give way to the light of Truth. And if you have the poise to keep still when unbelief is talking, the day will come when you will be intrusted by the Father with speaking or doing that which will reveal the real Jesus Christ and Him indwelling. Pray for understanding, for yourself. Get all your own faculties and powers

awake and working in perfect harmony with the
Christ pattern. You will be busy enough without bothering about what others are doing.

*        *        *

I smile as I think of your wanting to sit at
my feet—when you are ever in touch with the
Fount of all wisdom and understanding power
and life and love and substance! Your own indwelling Christ is beginning to find you receptive, and you will grow by leaps and bounds.
Never again be sad or give way to thoughts of
what might have been! Why, God is eternal,
unchanging good—you ever have access to all
that God is and has. And there's a Bible promise
that will help you to know that what may seem
lost is not so in reality, and that the opportunities
and blessings that seem gone will return just
as fast as you are ready for them. "I will restore
to you the years that the locust hath eaten,"
saith Jehovah. All that has been destroyed, neglected, or lost through lack of understanding
or foolishness or false pride or ambition can and
will be brought forth as present good just as
rapidly as you grow in consciousness; for God is
ever giving just what we expect!

# Jesus Christ

THE Unity teaching is based on the Jesus Christ teaching, and naturally we advise all people to hold firmly and steadfastly to the principles taught and demonstrated by this first Christian metaphysician. We have found in Christianity rightly interpreted more Truth than in any of the other religions we have dipped into; consequently we advocate it.

We have found Jesus to be the Great Teacher, accessible to all who have faith in and understand the spiritual principles that He sets forth. Jesus as a superman is here in our midst and we can every one of us receive instruction direct from Him if we ask Him, and agree to carry out in our life what He teaches. So if we want all that is contained in Christianity, Mohammedanism, and every other religion or religious cult that came out of Christianity, we should ask Jesus about it and He will show us the Truth just as fast as we develop our own spiritual nature to the point where He can import it to us. Jesus cannot reach the minds that are immersed in materialism. By those immersed in materialism we mean not only those who deal with the most material elements in the world but also those who have materialized Christianity.

To insure success and to inspire faith and confidence in ourselves and our undertaking, we should always have Christ as the source of our inspiration and prosperity. Our success and satisfaction in business, in home, in our social life is always greater when we take Christ Jesus as our partner; it is "Christ in you, the hope of glory." Why not follow in the footsteps of One who has demonstrated and proved every step of the way?

\*      \*      \*

God's love for us, for all His children, is so great that He sent Jesus Christ to be the Way-Shower to lead us to a greater realization of our heavenly Father's love and will for us. Jesus Christ is not merely a divine man who lived many centuries ago and whose life and works are to be considered past history. He is alive today. He is with us now. His words "Lo, I am with you always" is His living promise to each of us. The Christ presence within our own soul is the Great Physician who has wisdom and power to heal and to adjust in divine order every function of our body temple. Turning within to Him, we receive that guidance, that assurance, that healing for which our soul so longs, the prospering and success for which we not only long but so much need to express ourselves as a son of the Most High, heir to all that the Father has. Instead of thinking of the Lord as the personal Jesus Christ who is away at some distant place called heaven, we must begin to think of the Lord as our own God-given Christ mind, and of Jesus Christ as ever with us in the spiritual consciousness that He has established and that He has merged with the race mind in order that we may be in touch with Him and lay hold of Him and build our life according to His pattern.

There's a distinction between Jesus Christ, the man, and the perfect-man idea that God has created and implanted in each of us, His children. The Christ Mind is the crystal-clear mind that is not blurred by the "becoming" things of which the senses tell us, nor by the reports of the intellect which are records of man's experiments day by day. The Christ Mind gives us an idea in its entirety and then we work it out in our own consciousness and body and affairs.

For example, the Christ idea of love is given us, God love. Love unifies us with God, our source, and we know that we are good and true and fearless from within, because we let these God qualities well up from the center of our being. But love alone would not enable us to

keep our balance; it would draw us here and
there without regard to what we accomplished.
And here is where we begin to see the difference
between the man Jesus Christ as we know Him,
and the men who have fallen so far short of what
we term goodness and real power. Jesus exer-
cised all the God qualities we have yet been able
to discern in a masterly way. God love was expressed by Him; but it was supplemented and
balanced by God wisdom, and power, and judgment, and will, and zeal, and life, and renunciation, and strength, and order, and imagination,
and faith. Love drew Him to people; but good
judgment held Him to a course of action that
resulted in a success more far-reaching than any
of us have yet realized.

Jesus is the individual who made the com-
plete union of mind, soul, and body in Spirit.
He brought forth into expression the Christ, the
God-Mind within, and consciously identified
Himself with the Father. God is not a person;
"God is Spirit."

Jesus Christ has merged His wonderful consciousness with the race consciousness, that we
may turn to Him and receive into our own mind
the understanding of life and the activities of
mind that result in freedom from the limitations
of the race beliefs and the intellectual reason-
ings. We can each quicken our own Christ

Mind, by dwelling upon the Truth that we are one with Jesus Christ and one with God, through the understanding that Jesus the Christ helps us to unfold.

# Prayer

IT IS not enough to pray. Prayer is one step that you take, but you need other steps. You need to think of God, the all-powerful Healer, as being already within you, in every part of your mind, heart, and body. To keep one's attention and prayers in the spiritual realm of mind, without letting them work on out into the soul's expression and into the actual physical doing of that which corresponds with what the mind and heart has thought and spoken and prayed, is to court trouble. To keep declaring love and power and life and substance, and yet unconsciously, perhaps, assuming limitations and living them, will cause explosions and congestion that work out in the physical. We need to harmonize our thinking and our prayers with actual living experiences.

\*     \*     \*

Sometimes we pray to a God outside of ourselves. It is the God in the midst of us that frees and heals.

With our eye of faith we must see God in our flesh, see that wholeness for which we are praying in every part of the body temple. "Know ye not that your body is a temple of the Holy Spirit which is in you . . . glorify God therefore in your body."

Prayers aren't *sent out* at all! Sometimes that is our trouble. Where would we be sending our prayers? As individuals we should direct them to our own mind and heart and affairs. We commune with God-Mind within our own consciousness. Prayer is an exercise to change our own thought habits and our living habits, that we may set up a new and better activity, in accord with the divine law rather than with the suggestions we have received from various sources.

*       *       *

We sometimes think that we pray when we read and declare certain statements of Truth. We have very little idea of the way in which the answers to those prayers are coming. And we do not prove that we expect them to be answered. For almost immediately after praying we go on doing the things we have been doing, which does not allow of any answers. And we think and say that which is not in accord with the prayers we have made. For example, we go into the silence and declare statements of prosperity. Then in writing a letter we speak of lack

and failure and longing. Which proves that we
have those thoughts and feelings of lack in our
heart and that we are really dwelling on them
more strongly than we do on the Truth that we
have prayed.

Prayer, then, is to change mind and heart
so that God's omnipresent good may fill our
mind and heart and manifest in our life. If we
do not keep on thinking in accord with the
prayers we have made, we do not get good results. For all thought is formative; all thought
has its effect in our life. When some of our
thought energy is expended in negative beliefs
and feelings, and we show that we have old
mental habits in the subconscious mind, we
get those old negative results—even when we
are praying daily and when others are praying
for us.

We have a very decided part; we are to
cease worrying, and being anxious, and thinking and speaking of the past and of the apparent lack and idleness. We are to concentrate
all our attention upon the Truth of God, and
the truth of our own being, upon the very things
we would see taking place in our life. We cannot do this so long as we have negative thoughts
in our heart.

As we pray, the word of life is going down
into us, breaking up old fixed beliefs and re-

organizing our life. The word of life—life as God has planned it—is taking hold of our subconsciousness, and we know that we are free and will begin to use our freedom. Working in the consciousness of freedom, we will be happy and well and busy and prosperous. But our attention will be upon what we are doing rather than upon outer results. The results will take care of themselves once we have started our foundation in Truth.

"With God all things are possible." Those who receive spiritual help are the ones who place their undivided faith in God and who bring their thinking in line with His Truth. "Ye shall know the truth, and the truth shall make you free."

\* \* \*

Prayer, as Jesus Christ understood and used it, is communion with God; the communion of the child with his Father; the splendid confidential talks of the son with the Father. This communion is an attitude of mind and heart that lifts the individual into a wonderful sense of oneness with God, who is Spirit, the source of every good and perfect thing, and the substance that supplies all the child's needs— whether they are spiritual needs, social needs, mental needs, physical needs, or needs of a financial nature. Positive declaration of the truth of one's unity with God sets up a new current of thought power, which delivers one from the old beliefs and their depression. And when the soul is lifted up and becomes positive, the body and the affairs are readily healed.

\* \* \*

Sometimes I have written a letter to God when I have wanted to be sure that something would have divine consideration and love and attention. I have written the letter, and laid it away, in the assurance that the eyes of the loving and all-wise Father were seeing my letter and knowing my heart and working to find ways to bless me and help me to grow. So I suggest that *you* write a letter to God, telling, putting into words, that which your heart holds and hopes for. Have faith that God is seeing your letter and your heart, and that there is wisdom and power and freedom and love to accomplish that which will meet your needs. After you have placed your heart's desires with God, don't be anxious, or worried, or negative. Don't even be looking for signs that He has responded. Just busy yourself with the work He gives, and with study and prayer to develop yourself into a real companion and a real radiator of happiness and inspiration. As you do so you become the radiating center toward which those are drawn who will add to your happiness and cooperate with you in making of your life a beautiful success. Spirit intends you to be a radiating center that will draw to you whatsoever you need to be well and strong, successful and prosperous.

# Drawing On the Source

AN INDIVIDUAL who needs to realize and draw upon God's light and life and power and substance for health and sustenance, cannot make the grade so long as he is so situated that it is the way of least resistance to let others do for him that which they feel impelled, from love or any other motive, to do.

Each one of us is inseparably one with God, the source and substance of life and wisdom and every good. Each one must draw upon the source for his own sustenance, and for his own light, and for his own will power.

Parents too often claim the children who come to them as their own, and feel that they must think for them and do for them and take responsibilities for them. This is done until the child loses his God-given initiative and "lets down" and comes from habit to depend on others. This thought grows up with him, but all the time he resents this state of affairs, yet he has not developed the ability to launch out for himself, nor does he know that he possesses enough latent wisdom to work out of his difficulties.

Here is where God as universal law steps in and takes a hand. Where there has been failure to know and to measure up to the divine plan of life, circumstances arise, experiences come that make it necessary for the individual concerned to pull apart and to rely more and more upon himself.

If these individuals will make the most of such opportunities, and seek to develop from within the latent God-given resources and abilities, they will swing clear of the old entanglements and dependencies, and learning to draw on the source, they will bring forth their own God-given good. If an individual fails to see wherein he has transgressed the law of life and omnipresent good, he will continue to claim responsibilities that are not his and burdens that he need not assume and that hinder his own progress. He may through special prayer and effort realize a measure of harmony and health, but he will not know the fullness of good until he recognizes God as the omnipresent life and substance, ready to meet the needs of all His children in the way of Spirit and without burden or worry to any of them. Truth means little until it is applied to individual cases and needs.

\* \* \*

If a person would be healed and would keep

getting younger and more vigorous and alert
and ready for what the times demand of us, he
must wake up and get out of the rut, change his
habits, appropriate the life elements in food, in
the sunshine, and especially in Truth statements,
and prove that he is awake.

Instead of thinking about his apparent condition, of the race thought with which he may
have been struggling, or his age, he is to concentrate all his attention upon God, that he may
become so aware of His presence and His perfect pattern of life and His qualities that he
will forget old errors, and dissolve the conditions that he himself has built up from depen-
dence on something or somebody outside himself.

\*     \*     \*

God is the one perfect life flowing through
us. God is the one pure substance out of which
our organism is formed. God is the power that
gives us motive power; the strength that holds
us upright and allows us to exercise our members; the wisdom that gives us intelligence in
every cell of our organism, every thought of our
mind. God is the only reality of us; all else is but
a shadow that is cast by some foolish belief or
unwise combination of thoughts and the elements of being. When we let light flood us with

its sunshine, all clouds vanish and we begin to see ourselves in new ways of doing, which lead to wholeness and health and real satisfaction and growth.

The free flow of God's life through us becomes hindered in its expression if our thoughts and acts imply a belief in a limited number of years, in a hoarding of strength or substance or supply. We must prove here and now, for ourselves, our faith in God as omnipresent good and eternal life.

God in the midst of us is a great steady stream of renewing and cleansing and vitalizing life, and we can have the use of this life if we will open up the channels of its flowing and ourselves draw from this source.

\* \* \*

God has put in each of us the germ of immortality which will bring forth of its kind. "Every good tree bringeth forth good fruit."

So within us is this almightiness, like God, that we must cooperate with. As we do really cooperate with the Spirit of God in fulfilling His plan in us, all that is within us bursts into the beauty of wholeness.

The moment a person yields his self to God-likeness, he is letting the Spirit of God burst the shell of doubt and fear, and the light of faith reveals to him the light of life. He becomes conscious of the joy of life, the joy of life in himself and in everyone else.

Yielding self means giving up the old concepts of the past; forgetting ourselves and our human desire to come forth and just rejoicing that all God's creation does constantly spring forth in newness of life and light and joy and service. When we forget our own desires and really devote ourselves to doing what God would have done, this moment and constantly, we shall find that there is no limit whatsoever to the strength we have and the things we can do. We have yielded ourselves to the source and entered into a oneness that in itself makes us receptive to all that the source is and holds for us.

All God's blessings are for every child of the Father, and each individual should learn to receive direct from his indwelling source. Every individual has to live his own life and draw for himself upon the life, substance, health, strength that are waiting to be brought forth. No one can eat anyone's food for him, or breathe for him; neither can one person express the indwelling life and health for another. Each one of us must draw upon the source of these things for himself. Blessed are we when we recognize that this is the way of receiving, and do it.

# Going into the Silence

STUDENTS should not try so hard to "go into the silence." When your growth brings you to the place where your consciousness may be so completely merged with Christ ideas in God-Mind that you lose all sense of things about you, it is time to seek to go into the silence. But one should not try to hurry this experience. Anything that is an effort and that disturbs the natural functioning of the body is not going to bring your mind into conscious at-one-ment with the source of your light and every good.

It is because a person tries to force the process of going into the silence before he is ready for it, that he has that unpleasant experience, about which some ask, of the heart's beating so rapidly and hard. This comes from trying to get the body to become inactive in the effort to go into the silence. Instead of stirring up greater activity, laying hold of more life and using it, you cause the body to become tense. So the heart must pump harder to take care of its work. When wisdom and love and life and power prompt your thoughts, you are living and moving and having your being in the very presence of God, and you know that all is well. Then you will be able to concentrate upon anything that requires your attention, and you will be quiet and poised and comfortable. With a relaxed body you will lay hold of more life activity and come forth refreshed.

When you start to go into the silence, you should breathe evenly, in the happy feeling that you are taking in great drafts of God's pure life-sustaining air, which is being used by every cell and blood corpuscle.

Take your attention down out of your head into the organism. The flow of blood will follow the attention down into the trunk of the body and into the feet and hands, and thus the forces of being as well as the flow of the blood stream will be equalized. You should be just as fair to the members of your body as you would be to a neighbor. You wouldn't expect to hold the neighbor's attention on one spot all day long. Nor would you expect to demand of the neighbor that she do without something that she should have, nor would you burden her with more work than she should do. Now you are to treat your own members (which are close neighbors in your body temple) with just as much consideration and wisdom and love, giving them the benefit of this quiet time with the divine Creator.

*     *     *

A little period of quiet and rest each day is

your opportunity to establish yourself at the center of your being, the one place where the supply of life and substance is inexhaustible. God is this eternal life that we make into living. Each day you should have a regular period of stillness when the soul may gather sustaining power and restoring life. God gives freely; it is for us to keep the receiving channels open, to keep attuned to the realities so that this intellect of ours does not take us out among the limited ideas of the world. The manifest man must have the sustenance that can come only from within. We should not draw the strings of this instrument of Spirit so tight that the music of the soul cannot find expression, but this is what living in the world without withdrawal to the secret place does to us.

One can stay in the silence too much. It is merely the doorway opening onto that which is beyond the silence; i. e., activity based upon the light and strength gained in claiming it, accomplished by contacting it as the mind slips away from the clamor of dissipating thoughts. One can get too much of this good thing, just as one can get too much of perfectly good nourishing food, and then sit still, failing to convert it into living energy and the results of that energy. So, dear, watch that you do not remain too much alone, too much in the silence, too much in con-

templation and adoration, and not enough in
the practical use of what the walks and talks
alone with God would give. The Indian goes
solitary into the forest, on rare and stated oc-
casions, to gain a certain sense of his own su-
perior strength and poise. Then he comes back
to familiar scenes and regular activities, and
runs, and leaps, and rides, and sings, and plants,
and harvests, and tells the stories that inspire
his race, and ministers to those in need in the
spirit of love. He takes plenty of time to play,
and he works at nothing else while he's playing!

So instead of spending too much time in the
silence, begin to make real practical use of what
you have already gotten from study and from
the silence. It is possible to waste strength and
energy and substance in dwelling in that passive mental state sometimes called the silence,
or in the personal effort to make certain thoughts
go out and accomplish results that are not really
based on the divine order and plan of life. So
when you turn to the secret place for silence,
be sure that you get away from yourself, your
old ideas and desires, and bring your mind into
perfect harmony with the Christ ideas. Work
definitely to bring those ideas to bear upon your
thought centers, and then come forth to practice what you have just seen with spiritual vision
and declared for yourself.

The more you think about the Christ within, the stronger will grow your consciousness of the divine presence and your oneness with Him, until you can "be still, and know that I am God"; until you can still all the outer thoughts and meditate upon "Christ in you, the hope of glory." Many have been helped mightily, gloriously in finding the silence, by repeating the holy name "Jesus Christ" time after time, with short intervals between.

\* \* \*

When you go into the silence, it would be well for you to direct your attention down into your organism, away from your head. The flow of blood will follow the attention, and thus the forces of your being and the flow of the blood stream will be equalized.

You owe God attention. You owe Him the full measure of your faith, of your thought, of your service. He abides in your mind as the wisdom that will reveal the way to you if you will quiet your thoughts from their ceaseless outer searching for ways and means. He not only gives you wisdom, He is the wisdom that can direct you into paths of peace and plenty. You cannot listen to Him while your ear is given to your affairs. You can gain nothing by incessantly milling around in negative thought. You can gain all by quietly letting go of these outer appearances and laying hold of God.

You love Jesus Christ and He is now with you, guiding you and teaching you, bringing you consciously into oneness with the Father. His prayer was "That they may be one, even as we *are* one," His mission is to bring us into unity with the Father, and His promise is "Lo, I am with you always." He taught us to pray in this way: "When thou prayest, enter into thine inner chamber, and having shut thy door, pray to thy Father who is in secret." The inner chamber is that quiet place within the heart. We are taught to center our thoughts within, and then to shut the door; that is, to close our mind to all other thinking and think about God and His goodness and wonderful love; to pray to God in secret, in "the secret place of the Most High," and all things needful will be added.

"Speak to Him, thou, for He hears, and Spirit
        with Spirit can meet—
  Closer is He than breathing, and nearer than
        hands and feet."

That is what the poet says to help us remember how close and loving God is. Speak to God in the quiet of your heart, just as you would speak to me; tell the Father how much you desire to know Him and feel His loving presence and how glad you are to receive His blessings and to do

His will. Then be very still and just feel God's love enfold you.

\* \* \*

*Be still. Be still. Be still.* God in the midst of you is substance. God in the midst of you is love. God in the midst of you is wisdom. Let not your thoughts be given over to lack, but let wisdom fill them with the substance and faith of God. Let not your heart be a center of resentment and fear and doubt. Be still and know that at this moment it is the altar of God, of love; love so sure and unfailing, love so irresistible and magnetic that it draws your supply to you from the great storehouse of the universe. Trust God, use His wisdom, prove and express His love.

As you come out of the silence, count your blessings and give thanks for them. Realize that only the good exists in you and in your world, that the power you contacted in the silence may have opportunity to mutiply and increase your blessings. Give thanks that you have already received the good for which you looked to God in the silence, feeling the assurance "Before they call, I will answer; and while they are yet speaking, I will hear."

\* \* \*

On the "mountain top" we receive new illumination, inspiration, and insight into the providing law. Then we have a work to do away from the mountaintop, lifting all our thoughts to the Truth standard. We should carry the light, joy, peace, and strength we receive on the spiritual heights of consciousness down into our everyday life for the purpose of redeeming the human part of us.

Jesus had His times on the mountaintop, but afterward He descended to minister unto the needy ones. This symbolizes our habit of giving attention to thoughts of lack, weakness, negativeness and redeeming them by bringing them into the Spirit, after we have entered the "secret place of the Most High" and communed with the Father.

The thing to bear in mind is to take with you and hold on to all that you gain on the mountaintop of prayer, and not let go of it when you meet the thoughts and states of mind on the material plane that need to be spiritualized. In other words, maintain your spiritual poise and control when you meet adverse thoughts; otherwise you cannot redeem the Adversary.

When we seek God for Himself, all our temporal as well as spiritual needs are supplied. The providing law will always work for us when we work with it.

"Through wisdom is a house builded;
  And by understanding it is established;
  And by knowledge are the chambers filled
  With all precious and pleasant riches."
So it is through the development of our mind
that we find the way to success. God is mind.
"We have the mind of Christ," and it is for us
to make conscious union in the silence with the
all-providing Mind, lifting our thoughts to its
standard of Truth and holding them in this
Truth as we go about our own particular duties
of living.

# Quickened by the Spirit

YOU remember the spiritual inspiration that Paul had, an inspiration that is also ours as we claim the light and power and love that are God's expression through us:

"If the Spirit of him that raised up Jesus from the dead dwelleth in you, he that raised up Christ Jesus from the dead shall give life also to your mortal bodies through his Spirit that dwelleth in you."

It isn't individuals at Unity who quicken and heal. It isn't the human desire of the individual's own heart that makes the life to flow through his organism more freely. It isn't the thing that we usually think of as Christianity that brings one into the quickening, healing currents of Christ life. It is the stirring in us of the same Spirit of Christ that was and is in Jesus Christ —the Spirit of God, standing forth in individual consciousness and expression—the stirring up in our mind of divine ideas from the mind of Being. It is the soul's willingness and effort actually to live in its daily thinking and acts in the Spirit of Christ—that same Spirit which made Jesus to forget Himself in doing the good and perfect will of His Father. It is not church-going and praying and the observance of moral laws, but vital, loving, powerful words and acts of helpfulness to others. Jesus' consecration was a living, constant thing. He adored the Father and sought constantly to glorify Him in making the things of His Spirit manifest in the lives of His children. Jesus was eagerly discovering the real purpose of life and fulfilling it not for Himself alone but for all of us. And Jesus says: "Follow me." "If ye love me, ye will keep my commandments." "He that believeth on me, the works that I do shall he do also." "Feed my sheep." "As ye go, . . . Heal the sick, raise the dead, cleanse the lepers, cast out demons."

To be truly healed and quickened by the life more abundant, one must forget the past, and the limitations of the past, and offer every thought, every ounce of energy to Spirit, to be used in bringing God's kingdom of light and love and order and beauty and health into the earth, into the lives of all people. This giving is not to be done in human consciousness and might; but in the realization that it is God working through one's soul and body to increase constantly one's life and strength and substance, to fulfill His perfect plan. One's body is to be thought of as the temple of the living

God. One's arms and hands are to be thought
of, and used, as God's arms and hands, the expression of God-Mind's ideas of power and loving service and splendid work. The executive
power of the mind, in its relation to things that
we think of as belonging in the three-dimen-
sional world, is expressed through the arms and
hands. One should think of whatever one is led
to do as being God's work. One should know
and rejoice in one's innate ability to accomplish
that work. One should realize that one is free to
decide wisely, and to do whatever will benefit
oneself and others. One should see others in
this beautiful spiritual world of activity and
bless them.

God is in us as the very life and substance
that we use, and our use of His gifts increases
our ability to use and to direct them. God is
life, we make that life into living. God is love;
we make divine love into loving. God is substance; we take the substantial reality and bring
it through into the manifest world. God is wisdom; we claim oneness with divine wisdom and
it expresses through us as wise thoughts and
decisions and actions: the light of life that
glows from heart and face, yes, every cell of
the body.

# Understanding the Body

JESUS SAYS, "Ye therefore shall be perfect, as your heavenly Father is perfect." Paul says, "Your body is a temple of the Holy Spirit which is in you, which ye have from God . . . glorify God therefore in your body." Unity says, "God in the midst of you is mighty to quicken, to cleanse, to heal, to restore to wholeness, to prosper. Look within yourself, to the Christ Mind, for the light that will flood your soul and enable you to see yourself and your affairs in right relation to God and your fellows."

Seeing is the discerning capacity of the mind. By taking time for quiet meditation, and by confidently claiming oneness with God-Mind, we keep the avenues of our mind open to the divine plan for us. There is a divine law of mind action, that we may conform to, and that will always bring satisfactory results. Now, there is also a physical side to the operation of this divine law. The body and its needs must have our consideration. We must not drive the body or neglect its normal needs.

This body is the result of our use of God-given faculties and powers. We have needed such a temple, and the soul has built it. Sometimes we fail to remember that the temple is for the use of the Holy Spirit. Sometimes the belief in lack, or darkness, or time comes in to cause us to do things not good for the body temple. When there is evidence of disobedience, we should not seek to whip the body into submission and comfort by outer means or by mental treatment. We should prayerfully seek the understanding of the soul's need and bring ourselves into harmony with God-Mind.

Sometimes we become so intent upon some outer form of success that we keep our eyes fixed upon the partial good. Sometimes that which we undertake does not progress as we had dreamed, and we are tempted to see walls of limitation or the darkness of opposition. Sometimes in the effort to accomplish that which we feel we must do we are unfair to the body, until it calls a halt.

*       *       *

Whatever the cause of the appearance of negation, turning the attention Godward, with willingness to look into all phases of daily living and to make such adjustments as are wise and loving toward the body, will quickly relieve all strain and congestion and allow the free flow of life to renew nerves and structures.

The body responds to changes of mind; and when this is accompanied by truly wise living habits, the conformity to true ideas of life and power and love and substance and intelligence will renew it and make it every whit whole.

We must see the life of God in our flesh. Any form of denial of God life and intelligence or of the physical organism, any thought of the flesh other than as of God's pure substance, congests and irritates the body. This is double-mindedness, which consists in believing in evil as well as good, in perceiving and thinking about evil, or undesirable conditions, or lack, or failure, or calamity of any sort. Double-mindedness weakens the eyes and dims the vision, and we do not clearly perceive that which is our perfection in God-Mind.

To look about one and see evil and imperfection is sinful. That which we mentally stamp a thing is registered in our own flesh.

The eye is the outer evidence of the ability of the mind to discern and understand. A strong, unclouded, perceiving, and discerning mind attuned to Truth is manifest in strong, healthy eyes and clearness of sight; for one who perceives the Truth will live by the law of Truth.

\*　　\*　　\*

"I am God . . . the Holy One in the midst of thee."

God in the midst of us is mighty, and when we look toward Him in faith, He binds up, harmonizes, and strengthens whatever places need to be adjusted and restored. God, the Holy One in the midst of us, is that power which creates and is irresistible to renew and to make wholeness manifest. When we are full of faith and cooperate with this restoring principle of our being, God's work of restoration never ceases its activity in us. He seeks always to restore harmony, strength, life, wholeness in that which He has created. Our holding thoughts like these and communing with the indwelling Presence in the silence gives to the healing Christ within the best possible opportunity to do His work quickly. We do not at a time or renewal overtax the body and its energies, because we need to use the vigorous life of Spirit to build up our body temple. Let us pour out upon our organism blessings of praise for the good work it is doing in establishing wholeness. Let us think of ourselves as already manifesting perfection in mind, soul, and body, and give thanks that divine order *is now* established.

"I am God Almighty; walk before me, and be thou perfect."

The Father within is saying, "Be thou perfect"; and His word has fulfilled its mission of restoring the body with His own vital livingness.

# Day and Night Experience

*His delight is in the law of Jehovah;*
*And on his law doth he meditate day and night.*

THIS "day and night" does not mean, necessarily, the twenty-four hours of time. It has reference to the daytime of the soul—when it has light, and everything seems to be going smoothly, and it can see the evidences that the divine law is working; and to the nighttime of the soul—when a person has gone as far as the light of his own consciousness will take him in a given direction, and when he must turn within and wait for more light.

You may not see just how the law of the Lord is working for you, but it is working—just as surely as the law of growth is operative during the nighttime. The nighttime is necessary to the proper growth and development of plants, just as the daytime and sunlight with their warmth are necessary.

We wouldn't say that "business is dull" with the plants during the night or that they are not receiving their good. On the contrary, we have many times seen quite a transformation worked through the night. A plant that had seemed almost dead for lack of moisture and the ability to draw from the earth the required elements will be crisp and strong and very desirable in the morning! Had it not been for the night with its blessings, that plant would have ceased to grow and to yield its helpfulness to us.

When a nighttime comes to us, we should use it as a quiet time of great help. If we do, it will afford us time for meditation and the careful study of ourselves and our present methods and plan of service. It will cause us to turn more to the universal law and its operation and less to our own personal efforts and the ways of others.

In this nighttime we are to rest in the spiritual knowledge and assurance that our growth is precious in the sight of the Lord. We are to rejoice that the divine law is ever operative, ever working to prosper all of God's children. We are to give thanks that our affairs are in the Father's hands and under the management of divine wisdom.

Then we shall rise up to be glad for this "night" in which we have turned within to the great stream of light, and life, and love, and substance, and power, and have let them flow silently into the consciousness, to raise it to the

Christ understanding. As we do this, we will know that we are

"Like a tree planted by the streams of water,
That bringeth forth its fruit in its season,
Whose leaf also doth not wither;
And whatsoever he doeth shall prosper."

# No Incurable Disease

THERE is no such thing as a "disease" or incurable condition in the system. These activities, or weaknesses, or abnormalities to which the medical profession gives name are but the efforts of the God-given inner intelligence to deal with conditions that the individual has produced by his failure to understand the Truth and to recognize himself as the perfect child of God, and to live by the divine law of life. Anything that does not measure up to the Christ pattern of perfection can be changed. Anything that the ideas of God-Mind, expressing in the mind of man, have not produced can be dissolved into the original nothingness by the understanding application of the power of spiritual thought and the resultant spiritual action.

Doctors of course judge by appearances, founding their opinions upon the study of effects, and drawing their conclusions from the outworking of these mistakes which the patients have made.

No one who has awakened spiritually and is seeing his threefold being in the light of Truth would speak of disease as something of itself.

He would not think for a moment that the mind was fixed in old race beliefs or errors, nor that his body was unresponsive to the Spirit.

So when anyone comes to us who has had a doctor diagnose his illness, we ask him to turn deliberately from the doctor's opinions and verdict and cease even to think of the name he gave to the condition that existed at the time of the examination and treatment. We ask him to cast out and forget the assumption that this condition would not be changed and done away with utterly, just as one would refuse to hold and to think of some unworthy and untrue thing that he might have heard spoken as he walked down the street.

Then he is to begin at once to rejoice that he is the offspring of God, that the life and the substance of his body and the perfect pattern of that life and body are gifts of God, gifts that are in reality inseparably one with His own being, the very essence of God-life and God substance and God intelligence. It is God's plan, you know, to have the creation picture forth, express His own ideas, qualities, and being. And it is our purpose in being here to become conscious of and to express in our life the true pattern and qualities of our Father-Mother.

We know very well that God would not create a man with imperfections and shortcomings and diseased conditions. But we know also that He would not create automatons without free will and the privilege of exercising their powers of sonship. Just as we give our children —in our own thought of them and in our endeavors to have them live as they should that they may come forth clothed perfectly—the best that we can conceive, and then permit them to unfold their powers and faculties and their body temple as the inner intelligence and life prompts. We give them the best instruction we have to offer of course, but if we are wise, we permit the Spirit within them to develop the soul, that it may express the individual gifts.

So we accept the God-given perfection. We wave aside the past mistakes and the untrue suggestions, and fix undivided attention upon the Creator and the inner pattern of perfection. In this lies the success of spiritual treatment. We bring all the mental attitudes and the centers of consciousness, and even the physical structures, to this high place in mind where we see as God sees and where we name all that is within us according to the patterns and uses for which these soul qualities and their outpicturing have been created.

Then we prayerfully consider all our living habits to get a better understanding of their purposes and to know whether or not they are

really chording with the divine law of health.
We consider whether or not we are worrying or
fearing anything. We look back of the conscious
mind into the realm of the subconsciousness, or
memory, to determine whether there is anything that took place in the past that is contin-
uing its disturbing influence through the unconscious expressions of mind. Much of the
habit side of life is made up of these past experiences and trainings. Many things we do
daily are not consciously thought out but are the
continuation of something impressed upon us
long ago.

\* \* \*

So we rejoice and remember that we have
the God power to change conditions, the God
love to express Christlikeness, and we work
lovingly and diligently with whatever we find
in ourselves or our environment that falls short.
Keeping the attention centered in the Christ
Mind, we are able to see beyond the appearances
to the impulses of the soul, which is always
urging us in our efforts to make use of what
God has given. And to the degree that we let
Christ be lifted up, in the same degree shall we
rid ourselves of that which may have been pro-
nounced incurable or may have seemed to us a
disease that was incurable. Let us more and

more remember that which Jesus Christ said, "With God all things are possible," and let us listen until we hear within, "Is anything too hard for Jehovah?"

Any thought that is not based on the eternal reality, Truth, really has no existence at all. So if we *believe* in disease we are believing in something that has no substance or reality. When we dissolve the *belief* out of our mind and in its place establish the realization of the *one* presence and power of Good, and exercise our faith in *health* as the *one* presence and power within us, we shall feel the conviction that we are the expression of the health that God *is*.

This powerful conviction of oneness with divine wholeness will become abiding—nothing can take it from us. "God is love," and His love has cast out of the mind and heart all fear. There is no room for doubts and fears because God as love and health reigns supreme in us.

We set to work to change any and everything that we may find that does not measure up to the best that our new light shows us. We know that it is of much more importance to change and to do that which is really best for our progress and our health, than to be smugly consistent, or to make the excuse that we have always done a thing and that it is too late to change now. The moment we discover something undesirable in our mind or our life we should seek to make the changes necessary to bring the desirable into manifestation.

# Permanent Prosperity

THE only way to become permanently prosperous and successful is through the quickening, awakening, and bringing into righteous use of all the indwelling resources of Spirit. When we develop our soul and express its talents and capabilities in loving service to God and mankind, all of our temporal needs will be supplied in bountiful measure. We have access to the realm of rich ideas; we enrich our consciousness by incorporating these rich ideas into it. A rich consciousness always demonstrates manifest prosperity.

"The kingdom of God is within you." Jesus said, "Seek ye first his kingdom, and his righteousness; and all these things shall be added unto you." This means that we are to find the wealth of capabilities and spiritual resources within us, and bring them into expression. When we develop the power to accomplish things and the qualities that we need in order to accomplish them, our success is assured.

We must depend wholly on the *inner* kingdom of supply and the indwelling Christ, for this inner way is the only way to receive permanently. We are to cease depending on outer, material avenues for prosperity, because when we look to the outer we look away from the one resource that is within us.

Prosperity is the result of complying with definite laws that are revealed by the Spirit of truth within. Those who are prosperous and successful are the people who have a rich consciousness. They open their minds to rich ideas, and then cash in on these ideas in an outer way. The men who are famous and successful are the ones who have developed their innate abilities and used the success-producing ideas that have come to them.

Sometimes we begin at the wrong end of the prosperity line, and our methods need changing. Perhaps we try to accumulate money to meet our temporal needs without first laying hold of the equivalent of money on the inner planes of consciousness. This inner equivalent consists of our rich ideas, our innate capabilities and resources of Spirit.

One great help in realizing permanent prosperity is to come into the realization that we do not work to earn money to meet our expenses! This is a delusion of mortal mind. In reality, in earning money we are expressing the God-given faculties and powers to bless others, and to keep our part of the divine law of giving and receiving. The supply is a gift of God and is ours because it is a part of His plan. We are to accept it in faith as such. Expect it to come, and it will.

\*    \*    \*

Prosperity is not an accumulation of money or other so-called wealth, as we have sometimes thought. Wouldn't it really be a terrible thing if we were obliged to be eternally surrounded with the material baubles that we in our childish fancies believe to be prosperity? Wouldn't you dread to think of spending eternity, with chains of houses and lands, and storehouses of food, and wardrobes of clothing, and garages of cars, and chests of silver? Wouldn't you dread to think that men and women were always to be deluded with the belief that these formed things are the realities, the truly valuable things of life? Why, we'd always have to be employing guards and giving our thought to caring for our wealth! And we'd never get to the place where we could really get still and learn from the Father the deeper things, the soul-satisfying things—the lessons there are for us ere we arise into the majesty of sonship—the realization of oneness! Let us rejoice then that our resources are the God qualities, the spiritual sources and substances from which our consciousness, our body, our home, come forth in response to our need and our word of faith and wisdom and authority. Let us rejoice that our good is in the realm of Mind, where it is instantly available and responsive to our thought and word and need. Rejoice that it is all under law, that it holds us to the law, even though a negative attitude does fail to produce desirable results! The lessons of experience are helpful to us until we learn the unchangeableness of the law and determine in our own mind that prosperity is progress, accomplishment of that which one has an urge to do, gain in spiritual, mental, physical or financial matters, attainment of that which is good and needful. Supply in abundance for the so-called temporal needs is a part of prosperity. And surely, since God has given us this physical being, and the physical earth, and all its bounty, it is not wrong for us to get the understanding of the full free use of it all!

If we are ever to understand and use the higher spiritual laws, we must learn to use the laws governing our present state! As we do this, we shall see that they are really different phases of the same law.

"The Lord is more willing to give than we are to receive."

The bounty of God is within us, undeveloped, and all about us, unused and misunderstood. It is ours to use all that the Father has.

Did I hear you say that healing comes from the Spirit within but that prosperity comes from without, or is something outside? Well, now, are you sure? Let's see. Spirit within is the quickening, adjusting, harmonizing force, yes. We must agree to think health, and to bless the body, and to express that which causes all the functions of the organism to work perfectly. But there is the physical side of health, also? Spirit must have substance through which to manifest! You must provide the manifest substance and life elements in proper food, and drink, and sunshine, and air. Without these Spirit would have no vehicle—and these are drawn in from the outside! Do you see?

And so it is with prosperity. The Spirit of Christ in you reveals the plan of God in your life and quickens in you the urge and the desire for the activities and the appropriations that fulfill the divine law in your being. Your faculties must let Spirit work through them, and develop them to the point where they can express the Christ ideas. They must learn to draw upon the universal spiritual substance and life, and mold it, and make use of it either for health or for prosperity. We have accepted the suggestions of those whose judgments in other things we might not be willing to abide by, and have thought that some things are "food which perisheth." The consciousness determines whether it is food that perishes, or whether it is living substance that is building an eternal temple. The results we get from the full, free use of life and substance are determined by our beliefs and our habits.

When you develop your soul and express its talents and capabilities in loving service to God and mankind, all your temporal needs will be supplied in bountiful measure. You have access to the rich ideas of Divine Mind; enrich your consciousness by incorporating rich ideas into it. When you make righteous use of all your indwelling resources of Spirit, then you will become a magnet to attract success.

A splendid prosperity lesson is found in the 1st chapter of Joshua. "Only be strong and very courageous, to observe to do according to all the law . . . turn not from it to the right hand or to the left, that thou mayest have good success whithersoever thou goest. This book of the law shall not depart out of thy mouth, but thou shalt meditate thereon day and night, that thou mayest observe to do according to all that is written therein: for then thou shalt make thy way prosperous, and then thou shalt have good success . . . for Jehovah thy God is with thee."

When you "observe to do according to all that is written," the law will open all the ways and outer avenues of supply for you.

*        *        *

Those who take time regularly and who give themselves to the necessary prayer and meditation, to get new light and to round out their consciousness and ability to use all their faculties, find that they go from one prosperity to another. They frequently finish with one thing undertaken. This does not mean that they have failed or that they must be without position and resources. It means that they are being offered the next higher step, and that by entering upon the new undertaking or the greater light given in the present place, they are really growing and bringing forth more of the inner resources.

True prosperity is not making money, or putting out goods, or developing property. It is determining what our own individual soul requires in order to cause it to unfold more and more of God; and then how to harmonize its expression with the needs of our fellow men so that all are really benefited and inspired to unfold and express more of their inner spiritual resources. The exchange of merchandise and money is merely incidental to this spiritual association and growth. Money success comes as a result; but there are other results that should be sought and rejoiced over even more than the financial returns.

Radiant health and physical freedom and the greater awakening of all the faculties and their physical centers of activity is another more valuable gain than the increase in salary and the promotion to a greater chair in the management's office.

The feeling that one is doing something to help in the establishment of the kingdom of heaven in the earth is great compensation for the hours of prayer and the effort to swing clear of the old commercial bondage and ways. We are to have whatever we require, yes. But we are making progress toward the time when we shall work at something really constructive, something that reveals God in man and in His world, something that gives us the privilege of deciding for ourselves, under guidance of Spirit, when we are to go and when we are to come. As soon as we are capable of it, the Lord will place us in such a position among our fellows. But before we are given this place, we are to prove that we are ever considering the highest good of our neighbors, and that we have the ability really to discern what it is they need and bring them face to face with it. Spiritual growth, you see, as well as temporal ability and success!

# The Subconsciousness

**M**OST OF US have had to meet and deal with some of the subconscious holdings. Most of us have had so many years of arduous training in mortal beliefs, in the convictions of the intellect and senses, that we have very fixed subconscious states of mind, which have their correspondences in the activities of the soul and in the physical structures.

Wherever beliefs in materiality, in the power of disease, or in adversity of any sort have been allowed to settle back into mind, and result in formations of flesh or in functional activity, it takes great illumination—and not only illumination but earnest, constant identification of ourselves with Jesus Christ and His wonderful humility and obedience, and with the spiritual knowledge of mastering the physical elements—to dissolve and overcome and reform these beliefs. But as long as there is in our subconscious mind (our memory and habits of thinking) that which does not chord with Truth (God, good, the only presence and power in all and through all), we keep meeting it in some form or other, and we shall be obliged to keep using Truth and the power God has given us to change our mind if we are to cast out the old and establish a new order.

So long as we remember experiences that were unhappy, as we saw them once and still see them and speak of them, we shall be unable to demonstrate joy and real prosperity and health in our life. Because of lack of understanding these seemingly unkind things at the hands of others have made negative impressions upon our soul. And whatever has been impressed upon our soul will work out in our body and our affairs. Because the activities of the mind in its contacts with Divine Mind and also with the world of appearances and the minds of others, build the soul, which in turn forms the body through which it carries out its impressions and the urge from within; the soul's desires and impressions also make the conditions under which we live.

Understanding this law of mind action will help us to see just why we have the experiences we have, and why we have the reactions to them that we have, and why it is so important to keep going to God-Mind for more light and love and life and substance. We have power to change our soul's impressions, our subconscious, through the indwelling Christ Mind, and so change our body and its functioning and also the conditions about us.

It gives us renewed strength and confidence to realize that every thought of Truth that enters our mind is taking up its abode in our subconsciousness and is working itself out in our flesh as harmony and radiant health. Our body temple is the fruit of our mind. The truths that we hold in mind redeem and heal our flesh.

In Spirit and in Truth we are now and always every whit whole. By getting false thoughts out of the way, and keeping the image and likeness of wholeness ever before our mind's eye, and trying to *feel* that we are healed, health becomes irresistible and it is bound to manifest.

\*    \*    \*

When a soul is encouraged to develop the mental faculties and to open the heart to a great feeling of love for humanity, it just naturally opens up the subconscious door that allows it to peer into the past. For before we are entirely free from the shortcomings and the ignorance of the race mind, we must awaken to the fact that these things exist and that we are connected with them, until through the Jesus Christ Mind we swing clear of them and establish ourselves in a consciousness of life and light and freedom and love.

Now, we do not attain this place of life and light and freedom and love by allowing the soul to dwell upon these shadowy things of the past or by trying to recall the experiences through which we have come. Should we dwell upon such things, we should sink back into them. We must begin at once to rejoice in the light that is come to redeem our subconsciousness from the shadows of error and fear and superstition and mistakes. The race mind with which we are connected because of common experiences and beliefs suggests that we know not whence we come, nor where we go, nor yet how to direct our way along the path. Looking at life through this limited thought, it does seem gray, and we appear to grope our way and to leave much undone. But there is a new and wonderful way to view life; Jesus Christ lived so eagerly the light that came to Him day by day that life ceased to be a gray mystery to Him. He saw Himself and others in a new light. He understood why He had been born into the world. He knew where He was going. In fact, He knew that He was not going anywhere, in the sense of separation and distance, from us. He knew that He was merging Himself with the race mind so that He might abide with us and bring us into the same wonderful light in which He dwells.

When we cease to think shadows and lack of knowledge and begin to call to mind the teachings of Jesus Christ, we shall find the light shining for us. We shall not care to peer into the past, nor to recall its experiences. We shall know that all that measures up to the mark of helpfulness will abide with us. We shall be content to realize that when our growth makes it necessary for us to have something out of the subconscious, it will come without disturbing us, without depressing us.

The sensitive soul sympathetically attuned to the mind and feeling of humanity suffers greatly, when the mental vision opens, at exposing the soul to contact with the experiences of mankind during the past. For this very reason it is imperative that each Truth student should prayerfully seek to enter into the Jesus Christ consciousness of the omnipresence of God, the good. When we can look at life, present and past, through eyes that see only God and good, we can keep our poise. We see not frenzy of ignorance and anxiety, the mists of seeming failure, the gray of lack of love and wasted life. Rather we see the warmth and light of the great solar system that is of creative Mind's planning and that keeps working the miracle of growth; we see the radiance of the Son of God shining through the Son of man and men everywhere, perhaps a little here, a little there, but shining surely to bring forth the fruits of His planting.

We are the children of the Creator of this wonderful universe.

I do not believe that the lily feels the terrors of darkness down at the bottom of the pond, nor does it allow the mud and water that shut out much of the light to keep it from appropriating the good that is provided for it, and pushing surely and intelligently upward to the freedom and light that were there for it long before the bulb began to swell and to burst. I am sure that the lily is "conscious" only of the foods in the earth and the warmth and helpfulness of the sun and air.

I am sure that if we allow the intelligence within us to appropriate only the good and that which keeps us looking up, we too shall be conscious of good only, and we shall grow just as perfectly as the lily.

I am sure that if we do as Jesus suggested, turning to the Holy Spirit (the whole Spirit of God) and seeking to know the good only, we shall grow just as surely and as perfectly into the Christ consciousness as Jesus did. I do not say that we can take our frequently translated Scriptures and depend on them entirely for our instruction and guidance. But we may depend

always on the Holy Spirit of Jesus Christ, which
is ever here with us, to give us whatever we
have need of from time to time.

# Threefold Healing

TWO of your statements prompt us to a little explanation, before giving the outline for treatments: (1) "I am wondering if you will send me, also my brother, some health vibrations." (2) "We are asking you to relieve us through the Silent Unity healing." We are not just sure that you understand that you are to cooperate with us, by studying the Truth so that you may come into the understanding of the divine laws of health and life and prosperity, and by joining us daily, regularly, in prayers that we shall suggest.

We will not say that the work we do here has nothing to do with the healing. But we do not promise results unless we have the faith and the cooperation of those for whom we pray and to whom we give instruction. For after all it is not the physical and mental relief that means most to the persons receiving treatment, and we are not so much concerned with the *results* as we are with the growth in consciousness that will make the results abiding.

This health law is threefold: spiritual, keeping a person assured of his God-given freedom from all anxiety and worry and fear and lack; mental, giving him the intelligence that enables him always to do that which promotes health and success; physical, forming those habits which keep him making the right use of all his faculties, and powers, and the life energy and substance.

There is a tendency these days to disregard the harmonious combination of these three elements, one person being very careful to observe the spiritual, another to accomplish results through the physical. Our work is to unify these three and to bring our students into the understanding application of the Truth of being.

One who remembers and lives by the spiritual promises of the law of health will not worry, or seek to manage other people's affairs, or neglect to feed his own soul with that which is necessary to keep it unfolding Christward.

One who is aware of the mental side of his health seeks to keep himself free from the limitations of the race mind, the opinions and demands of others, the depressions and hurried attitudes that keep the Christ ideas from finding perfect expression through his thoughts and acts.

One who is determined that his physical life shall show forth the peace and order of the spiritual reality and the divine intelligence is considerate of his body, and careful in his demands upon it. He sees to it that he understands the physical requirements and that he meets these every day.

So you see there is more to our Silent Unity ministry than a formula of words to be said at intervals! We want to help you to live the Christ life here and now, which means to live a life of understanding trust in the good; of joyous activity, mental and physical; of freedom from fear and worry; of loving contact with your fellows, without anxiety as to their apparent shortcomings or selfishness. So we ask you to consider prayerfully the following explanation of your being, and to seek to incorporate an understanding of it in your consciousness, using it in your daily living.

Being threefold, spirit, soul, body, we find that our expression also is threefold, the harmonious and constructive unfoldments are threefold, and the things that we term undesirable and imperfect and destructive are threefold also. For example, joyous radiant health is the result of the right *spiritual* viewpoint, the daily purposeful effort to unfold the faculties and *soul* qualities, and the daily recognition of the *body* as the temple of God and the structure that Spirit and soul are building, all these prompting us to give careful attention to the needs of the system. And weakness, or sickness, or inharmony, or imperfection in the organism, is the result of some failure to identify oneself with God, the divine source, and understanding how to lay hold of and express one's inheritance of *spiritual* powers; some limitation in the *soul's* development of its riches; some ignorance of the *body's* requirements and disregard of the divine law of life and health.

Definite study and training are required for righteous expression of our threefold nature. The study and training should be more thorough than are our first lessons in life, because we are dealing with advanced stages of the same thing. Because of lack of understanding much must be done over and changed. So if we would have the full, free use of our senses and our organs, we must get at the causes of the inharmonies, remove them, and establish a new and perfect pattern and plan of action. We do this by remembering that we are God's children, that He has created us perfect, and that there is a law established within us that will keep us unfolding harmoniously if we will but recognize it.

We who have begun it find this study of the Truth of being and the science of living much more fascinating than any school course.

To know how to hear with the mind, and to discern and discriminate between the true and real and worth while and that which is mere foolishness and the clatter of elements not yet organized under law; and to realize that one may be obedient and receptive without giving up one's own right to freedom of choice and action, is real accomplishment.

To know how to see with the mind, to discern and to understand that which the nerves and cells of the sight organs report without being disturbed by the masses of manifest substance and the actions of those about one, gives real joy and poise. And the eyes themselves are kept strong and steady and equal to the work for which they were formed.

To know how to detect that which is adverse and not for one's good and to refuse to bother oneself about the seeming errors, so that the mind may be free to think out and to register only good, and the nose (the organ that the mind has built to help it in its work of taking in that which is required and of leading the body into pleasant experiences only) may be kept clean and open and keen to respond.

To realize that one has God-given capacity for judging righteous judgment and to understand that this judgment can and will keep one from bitter experiences and enable one to discriminate in all things, is one of the greatest blessings we have. The faculty of judgment has

built the sense of taste, and when we are giving
the attention to this faculty that we should, our
taste helps mightily in the care of our body.

There are the other senses, which are equally
fascinating and perhaps more subtle. But this
is enough to show just what we mean by spiritual study, which re-educates us and enables us
to go on from where many of us have stopped.

*        *        *

Daily declare that your spiritual life and
world, your mental life and world, your physical life and world are unified and that you are
expressing harmoniously the ideas of the Christ
Mind on these three planes. Know that your
everyday physical life can and should be inspired and happy and purposeful, yet not
strained and tense, and that it is never necessary
to do that which is harmful or weakening to
any of the functions or organs in accomplishing
what is right and just and worth while and ex-
pedient. As you practice mentally seeing God's
plan and world in your life, you will find that
you are better poised, that you will do just the
right thing, and that your body will be healthy.

The realm of mind is even more fascinating
than the manifestation of its ideas. One who
strikes a balance between the study of the mental side and the manifestations, and in living in

his threefold being is truly blessed. He is free, and joyous, and can keep healthy and prosperous. The past does not worry him, the future does not entice him; he knows that a full measure of good is his, here and now. He profits by the past, glories in the now, and is fearlessly looking toward the future!

# Developing Our Faculties

THE ONLY way to abide in cosmic consciousness is to develop Christ consciousness, the abiding realization of oneness with God-Mind and of its ideas as directing all the faculties in fulfilling the divine purpose in being.

All true followers of Jesus Christ are required to discipline the human self in the journey from the personal to the Christ consciousness. The human part of us wants to cling to things visible and to other people, but as the impersonal, spiritual, Christ finds expression we gradually cease to lean upon these material limitations. Our spiritual faculties become so strong, vital, and substantial that we are able to contact the great invisible through them. When these faculties are well developed, the invisible reality becomes to us even more real and substantial and enduring than material things are to the senses.

We study God as mind, and man as mind; and we find that in the expression of divine ideas man has definite centers of consciousness, which the soul has built through its effort to use the divine ideas or qualities of being. We have found that there are twelve central or basic centers of consciousness, which are the result of the soul's use of the God qualities of life, and love, and wisdom, and power, and substance. These centers of consciousness are centers of God-Mind; but they have built the physical organism through which they express. So we have twelve locations in the body, where the soul expresses definite qualities, which go to make up the Christ consciousness—at least we term it Christ consciousness when the individual is expressing himself under divine law. Developing these latent powers and capacities of the inner man is the key that will open to us the kingdom and give us Christ mastery. When we do this we shall succeed in whatever we undertake.

None of us are yet able at all times to keep our faculties expressing perfectly. But we are finding out that we can discipline ourselves and call upon the Spirit of God to act through us, which is the light that is given to every one of us as we come into being and that gives us whatever we need in the way of love and wisdom and faith and understanding and zeal, and the life and strength, the power and the will and the imagination to carry out the divine pattern and in an orderly way to eliminate or renounce all that has not been implanted in us by the Father.

*        *        *

In the development of faculties and powers —talents—in self-expression through them, and in the service to others that one must consider, in order to be truly successful and satisfied one must go to God-Mind to learn what is truly best for the soul at the time. Sometimes a soul will get into a rut through the desire to excel in some particular line, disregarding development along other lines.

We need all our faculties awake and alert to discern the reality of Being, and to see through the be-coming things to the underlying cause and to eventual order and perfection. We find that a daily development of all our faculties keeps us better balanced.

*        *        *

Faith and love are qualities of Divine Mind that bring the individual into close communion with the Father and source of all light and blessings. Having quickened faith and love, one may go a long way on life's path and solve many problems. But eventually the very quickening of these two faculties of the soul will call for a full-rounded development.

Faith and love will prompt a person to

identify himself with the best he knows in religious life. This brings him to a realization of the need of developing more and more of the Christ powers; also the need of giving up the old race beliefs and human fears and personal ambitions. All that does not measure up is left behind as he follows Jesus Christ in calling and educating his disciples or faculties.

Love without the cooperation of wisdom and good judgment and will would not give us the well-rounded expression that we desire, yet purified love will make it much easier to direct these other faculties into accord with the Christ pattern.

You speak so often of love, and of the importance of love, and the necessity of love in healing; and that you make many affirmations of love and power. Well, now, wouldn't it be well to remember that there are a number of other qualities equally important, and that the development of these others is just as necessary as is the exercise of love? God is love. But God is also life, and power, and strength, and substance.

Love is little more than affection and animal devotion, until other faculties are developed to the point of enabling the individual to see and understand in others that which is loved. Faith must be active; discrimination or judgment must help one to see the real and to understand that which appears perhaps unlovely; imagination must picture the God qualities in one's fellows and in one's environment that are lovable; understanding must keep the love from becoming negative or selfish; will must hold one to a true course and to that which the good judgment indicates as best; renunciation plays its part in that it helps us to give up that which would hinder development. Strength must be recognized as from within and be so established that it supports every other faculty.

\* \* \*

Sometimes in our zeal for the Lord's work as we feel called to do it we emphasize the negative side of life and substance and love until we draw about us the correspondences to those negations. For example, a great desire for purity and for helping others to know and live pure lives may cause us to throw so much of our thought energy and substance into the fight against so-called impurity and waste and weakness that we fail to have enough energy and substance to build up our own life and to create the loveliness that is God's plan for us.

When everyone seeks to live in perfect harmony with the divine law, he will begin to see order in his life and discord, if there is any,

will be the unusual thing. In fact there will be
nothing but order, harmony, and perfect conditions when we learn to express our Christ self.
First and last one must understand and appreciate life and lay hold of the life faculty in
such a way as to keep a vital interest in living
and in bringing the body to its highest point of
development—not necessarily to a given number of pounds nor to a given strength, nor to the
point where it heeds merely the demands of the
personal will and ambition—but to the goal of
the radiant health and freedom that come of
living from within, in harmony with the inner
intelligence and the Christ pattern.

\* \* \*

The light of Spirit, quickening the understanding, sets us free from all mortal sense and
the boundaries placed by intellect. In the light
of understanding we behold God's presence,
and His kingdom, and His children, and we see
all these as one, and each in right relation to
the others. The faculty of discrimination enables
us to know if we have really awakened and
developed the capacity for righteous judgment
and harmonious expression and Christlike attitude along all lines.

It is merely a matter of giving up the lesser
to receive the greater. So long as our mental

hands and our soul forces are holding us to limitations to the personal, there is no room in them for the mighty blessings of Spirit that the development of the faculties through selflessness will bring.

The human part of us goes through a "crucifixion," and our spiritual, Christ self is resurrected. Whatever is good and true within us is not crucified—it does not need to be. Whatever is good endures always and becomes one with the Christ in us.

# Spiritual Control of the Body

UNITY does emphasize control of the physical by the spiritual. But many of the things that we do and expect to control are not spiritual in the sense that they are in accord with God's laws and plans! The real control is in living according to the perfect pattern and law. It is not spiritual thought that prompts one to abuse the body in any way. It is not spiritual thought or desire that allows one to eat when there is no need of food, or to partake of food elements that are not what the body requires at the time. It is not spiritual thought that causes one to worry, or to become tense, or to drive the body in the effort to gain intellectually.

A thing is not less spiritual because it has taken form and weight and color. The thing that might be termed "material" is the misconception or unwise combination of thoughts and elements, that produces an undesirable result. Spirit becomes manifest in man's expression of what God gives.

Our religious life, heretofore, has led us to feel that our thoughts and our emotions were all that was necessary to our spiritual experience; that the body was to be disregarded as of little consequence and as really not responsive to the finer things of Spirit—at least not as anything of importance except as "controlled" by them.

Evidently, the individual soul has felt the need of just such an earth home as the body temple. We are to realize that the body, free from the inharmonies and weaknesses imposed upon it through error, is a part of God's plan of life. We understand man to be a threefold being. Just now we are convinced that the regular appropriation of certain manifest life elements is required to maintain the body at a given rate of vibration—which we know as health and endurance and ability to transmute thought into action. We do not know how long such a plan will be in effect; we are not greatly concerned. But it is reasonable to suppose that we shall not learn a great deal about laws and manifestations in advance of those which are now receiving our attention until we have learned to live by them. When we can sustain the body in health and activity and radiance indefinitely, we shall have gained a better understanding of the true purpose of life and will be ready to enter upon a mode of living that may free us from the observance of laws that we may term "physical." The science of building and operating an airplane would not permit the builder and the mechanics to take just any materials at hand out of which to fashion the parts of the plane or to furnish it with fuel. Yet we know that the power to build and drive the machine is in the builder's mind and in the universal atmosphere. Nevertheless, knowing this and acting upon it, we do not seek to set aside the laws revealed by intelligence as expressed in the working of machinery and the settled mode of travel.

Man learns to build an airplane in which to fly before he is intrusted with the higher law of taking his body through the air without a manifest vehicle.

Building the planes and using them and observing the laws governing their flight is not denying God's spiritual laws. It is taking the steps that are leading him forward to the discovery of greater things.

And so it is with maintaining ourselves in health, and in studying and applying spiritual rules of action. We must learn to make the right use of what we have—and then we shall find ourselves in possession of more.

\*      \*      \*

Sometimes, the soul gets so anxious about what it wishes to do that it tends to neglect the body. This is not fair to the body nor to those who must take care of the body when it is neglected. Our first duty, then, is to bless our body and to get our thoughts right down into it, to praise its wonderful work, to learn what its needs are, and to arrange for supplying them. Sometimes things happen in the realm of the senses or in connection with the physical body that cause one to depreciate it, or even to almost wish one did not have it. And in this event the soul may reach out so much that the body is neglected, until it suffers.

Then we sometimes become too ambitious, somewhere in the recesses of the soul, and literally pull ourselves up by the roots, and starve the precious body temple. Then come hard experiences—blessings in disguise.

But God is there in that body, you know, and He won't let the soul continue to neglect the body. Suffering is one of the means of drawing the attention of the soul back to its beautiful temple. And the Christ Mind can and will direct the soul in taking up its wonderful work in the body that it may continue to have this very necessary vehicle of expression.

We need more often to think of our body as being the temple of divine love, the very substance of health and harmony in order that this truth may be implanted in the subconscious mind, which controls the body functioning. We need more often to pray for a true concept of substance, for with it we shall receive a glorious revelation that will go a long way toward transforming the mind, soul, and body. This concept of substance will be but the beginning of a transformation that will continue until we shall be able to demonstrate as Christ Jesus did. All who follow Him will eventually overcome as He did, spiritualizing the soul to the extent that its outer garment, the body, will be lifted into a like expression of Spirit; for God is no respecter of persons.

# The Way to Health

PAUL said, "Be ye transformed by the renewal of your mind." In renewing the mind and bringing it into accord with Divine Mind, in which we all have individual consciousness, one needs to understand the character of the one Mind and the Truth of being as the Creator has established it. Then it is well to understand where one has been making mistakes, judging by appearances, accepting illusions, working contrary to Principle, using the faculties in ways not intended by the Creator. These mistakes and misuses of one's God-given faculties are what we term the causes of human inharmonies. The change of causes also changes the effects.

When the individual keeps his mind in tune with God-Mind, he knows constant harmony, and order, and success, and health. By following the teaching of Jesus Christ and seeking guidance of the Most High he does not leave room for a negative thought to enter. Health, or harmony, is the one presence and the one power in the universe.

The Creator is continually doing His work of restoration throughout His creation, especially in every man and in every woman, for He put all His children into the world to manifest His wisdom, harmony, joy, health, perfection—all that He is.

When we learn how to cooperate with this all-powerful Spirit of restoration, nothing can stand in the way of our manifesting the health that belongs to us by divine right.

During periods of communion with the Father in the Holy Spirit, it is possible for the individual to know the way of peace and prosperity and freedom from all condemnation or anxiety or injustice, and the way of health and continued strength and youth. Study of Truth, prayer for greater realization of Truth, brings one into this divine order described above. This is the rebirth spoken of in Scripture, and is the way into the kingdom.

All this may seem at first glance to be a roundabout way to health, but it is really the most direct way to health and all other good. We as individuals lose health, or peace of mind, or other desirable states by our failure to know how to identify ourselves with God the Father, and to use His gifts to us, and to let Spirit express through all our faculties and powers.

First of all, in seeking a way to health we need to see clearly that God is omnipresent, as omnipresent as the very life in which we live

and move and have our being; as the very substance out of which our body is formed and
nourished; as the very intelligence that is within
us, in every nerve and brain cell and structure
of the body; as the very love that draws together
and holds in perfect harmony (if we will only
allow it) all the elements of our being; as the
very light that radiates through us to bless and
help others, the light that enables us to understand ourselves and others and all God's creation, so that we may always think the Truth,
the true state of all the creation.

*        *        *

Whenever we have an experience of sickness it is evidence that we have been letting go
of our hold on the gifts of God. We have ceased
eagerly to appropriate and analyze and assimi-
late and make use of the life of Spirit through
our thoughts, our words, our acts, our living
habits.

We need to stir up and quicken our senses
and give them the baptism of the new life in
Christ Jesus. Our organism has been asleep from
disuse and lack of real vital interest in living—
not merely in eating and drinking and sleeping
and being entertained—but in the vital issues
that have to do with bringing ourselves into the
full-rounded Jesus Christ expression of life.

In seeking the way to health we are to pray for an understanding of our oneness with God, to claim it. We are to study this relationship so that we may know how to lay hold of the abundant life and intelligence and substance and love of God, and build these into our soul and our body, that we may perfect our expression.

The eyes are the physical organs that are the outpicturing of the capacity of the mind to discern, mentally, physically, spiritually, all that is. Seeing is a mental process; and the eyes are the instruments that register what the mind has been trained to think and to behold. When our mental processes are in perfectly harmonious accord with the ideas of Divine Mind, our sight is perfect and our eyes function properly, with nothing coming between to hinder.

The ears represent the instruments of the mind through which we receive instruction from God's mind. Hearing is the receptive capacity of the mind, and only as a person is open and receptive to the voice from within and willing to be guided in all ways and at all times by this voice of wisdom, is his hearing sense lifted to the spiritual plane and being put to the use God ordained it should have. Listening within for the still small voice with a mind consecrated to obedience trains the ears to their true function.

The nose is the physical organ that is the outpicturing of the detective capacity of the mind. The sense of taste is also mental in reality, discriminating, appropriating. The senses are built to enable the mind to function in its capacity to find that which is good for the soul and body, and to direct the individual toward the appropriation of it. The mind that is in tune with the true being, the Christ self, is not interested in ferreting out evil, nor in dwelling upon the undesirable in any way.

With our feeling sense we are to feel for God, keep our attention on Him and train our faculties, senses, emotions, feelings to comprehend His radiations, His qualities as they express in man's consciousness and body and affairs. Then do we feel God, His presence of love, life, joy, wisdom, power, and the expressions of these God ideas so positively and so fully that we are quickened, and radiate the very things our mind holds so that our world too feels the presence of God.

* * *

The one who is truly seeking that which is of God is expressing the good and the true in thought. He does not think adverse thoughts, nor believe in impurity of any sort in the self or in others. And so this sense of smell and the sense of taste are powers of God-Mind, which is ever working to connect us with our good.

Baptizing the senses of seeing and hearing and smelling and tasting and feeling leads to natural intuition and spiritual insight and the power to identify ourselves with the absolute (God, the good). All the senses work in the realm of mind, but all have their physical side and use. We use what they tell us in our thought world. That which we think of ourselves or of others, or of the creation in general, we build up the belief in and begin to register in our own soul and body. That which we habitually see mentally, our eyes begin to visualize, and the cell structures of the organs themselves are affected and built according to the vibrations set up by the thoughts. This is true of the other senses and their organs. Our negative thoughts and emotions (feelings) react upon the parts of the body that have to do with phases of life that they touch.

\* \* \*

The way to healing is first of all to re-educate the mind and to establish the Truth in all the faculties; then to see the reality of the body and its functions and to stamp every part with the perfect pattern, which is God-given and known as the Christ man, the out-picturing of the Christ ideas in individual consciousness; then to study the living habits and make them conform to the truth that good only is real and abiding and truly active.

Heretofore the individual may have gone to physicians and surgeons to receive their suggestions and treatment. He now goes to God-Mind, which the Holy Spirit promised by Jesus Christ makes known. He holds to the truth that his body is pure and alive and perfect in every part, because he wishes to use this perfect mental pattern to direct him in his treatment. He then looks into all his thought habits to see that they are prompted by faith and divine love and wisdom and life and joy and freedom. He looks into his living habits to see that he is really taking good care of the body and meeting the requirements of its many departments and functions. He acquaints himself with the different parts of the body, and learns what it is they are truly built for. He learns what each needs and supplies them.

He formulates prayers based on the Truth of his being, and uses these prayers faithfully in order to feel them in the mental side of his body. He realizes that he is re-educating his mind and that he is reforming the physical structures.

*       *       *

God not only has created the earth and us, but He is actually the very essence of all that we see about us and all that is within us. We are the free agents, who must learn to take and combine His ideas and the manifest materials into the soul and body we are to use. We are not sitting off here doing something by ourselves and occasionally asking God, outside of us, to help. In reality God is working out through His offspring that which He has conceived to be the ideal creation and life. But He has given us the power that He is, just as any wise father gives his son full freedom to become the son he feels sure that son will be. He gives him the best start he knows how to give and then leaves it with the son to use his heritage, to make his own way in life. And that is just what God is doing with us. When we ourselves make health, wholeness, holiness the dominant thought of our mind, re-educating all our physical senses to their true purpose, our body temple will be sure to manifest its God-given perfection, because our body is the fruit of our mind.

Thus we remake our consciousness so that it will correspond with God's perfect idea of us. Our part is to consecrate all our senses to the Truth and train our thought children to express joy, love, faith, wisdom, life, health.

# Helping Others

INSTEAD of thinking of the people whom you have believed to be evil and an undesirable influence, begin to think of the goodness of God in the life of all His children. Think of God as everywhere present light, and love, and peace, and power, and life. Think of all men, all women, all children as ever abiding in His presence and expressing His qualities. As you do this, you will touch the reality of individuals, and you will invite only the best from them. Spirit will respond as you expect it to, for the Spirit of God is in each and every person. Some persons have not yet wakened to this realization; but as you declare the Truth for them and expect to have it express through them toward you, you will receive only loving and considerate treatment from them. As you read these explanations of the way in which a soul may lay hold of its inheritance from God and exercise its God-given freedom in the endeavor to develop and use its powers, pray for more light to enable you to see just how precious these individuals are and how important it is that we all have freedom to correct our mistakes.

The best way to help your brother is to pray for him to be spiritually illumined. Then if he has come to a place in his soul development where he is ready to accept Truth, he will have the understanding and desire to seek the indwelling Christ.

It is never wise to try to force Truth upon anyone. Place your brother "lovingly in the hands of the Father," and know that his own indwelling Lord will take care of him until he is open and receptive to ideas of Truth.

\* \* \*

You are good, yes. But it is a negative goodness. You haven't realized your powers and made positive and purposeful use of them. You have been made to feel that nonresistance, and righteousness, and Christianity, and loving service are all passive. You have allowed your personal ideas of love and good will to make you too sympathetic and inclined to give, without seeking and asking for wisdom and good judgment to direct you.

Now while it is a virtue to be always ready to help others, we must be sure that we are truly helping them, and not hindering them by allowing them to continue in the unwise habits that have brought them to lack.

The greatest help is to be able to show others

how they may help themselves and become self-supporting and resourceful. Study and prayer, along the lines of the Unity literature, will give you the knowledge and power really to help others to understand and bring forth their prosperity.

You have a store. Have you taken God into partnership with you? Do you start every day with quiet, purposeful communion with God? Do you really ask God to show you just what to do in each and every transaction?

Do you bless your store—the room, the stock of goods, the accounts, the customers, the salespeople? Do you fill the atmosphere with thoughts and words of love and wisdom and prosperity?

Do you demand of others that which you demand of yourself, that they use good judgment, and self-denial when necessary? Do you make them understand that God prospers those who do their part; and that you expect them to do their part to pay their bills, so that you can pay yours and go on with the store, the service you feel led to offer?

Or do you think of the sickness, and the poverty, and the inharmony about you? Do you let folks have merchandise because you think them in need, or because they are God's children, and you are in this way helping Him to prosper them and make them happy; and because your business is going to prosper all and result in greater blessings? Do you pray for their prosperity? Do you expect God in these people and God in you to prompt them in doing that which is right by you?

By studying this matter you will come into a better understanding of the law of prosperity and you will be led into a much happier and more successful handling of your everyday problems.

Don't feel that you must just open your hands and pass out everything that you have. Conservation is one of the rules of success. You must expect others to do their part. And everyone, no matter how many failures he has had, can do his part.

\* \* \*

You aren't really giving Spirit much credit for ability to work in your brother's consciousness and affairs, are you? You say in the same breath that he has been upheld by the Spirit these months and that you feel he cannot stand the strain much longer! Don't you see what a mixed state of consciousness that is, and how foolish it is to pray and to expect Spirit to express its harmony and order and light in yourself or another, and then to feel that you or the other may at any time collapse because of the lack of spiritual power or light or life or substance?

Suppose "his mind," this tense, mortal state of mind that has been causing him the worry and anxiety and weariness, does give way! What then? Why, that's the very thing that must come! This old fixed state of mind must give way, or be given up, that the Christ ideas may flow freely through his consciousness and give him the new life and light and poise and power and substance that he needs! Encourage him to let go, to place himself in God's care and keeping. It is personal assumption of responsibility that makes him feel he must cling so tenaciously to some of his opinions and ways of working. This is the only thing that keeps him out of the kingdom of heaven and its blessings! The treatment he has had, if he were cooperating, would have raised him into the Christ consciousness of peace and order and success long ago.

We are asking you to place him confidently in the care and keeping of his own indwelling Lord and to take your mental hands off! Don't even treat him! So long as you are trying to force something into him, you keep his attention divided, and he doesn't really get within and quiet enough to let his own soul commune with God. Leave him in the secret place, with the Father. Jesus has promised, you know, that those who go to the Father in secret, shall be rewarded openly!

The spiritual light coming to him from within will show him the utter foolishness of struggling and worrying and striving. It will reveal to him the right relation of things spiritual and things manifest. And he will see clearly how the right mental attitude and physical poise and health will result in instant and constant progress and prosperity and satisfaction. You can't give him this. Nor can we. It is the free gift of the Father within him.

\* \* \*

What are you believing about this Father, who Jesus Christ proved was willing always to hear and to answer every call in the name of His Son Jesus Christ?

You are looking for a call. Do you really know when you are called? You are to go straight to God to talk over these things. Go into your closet of prayer, into your "secret place of the Most High" and *shut the door;* then really pray.

We are not promised the Father's attention when we merely moan and cry out, "Oh, I long so to do something for this ailing one." Did Jesus Christ perform any healing by wishing that He had the power? No. God gave Him the power; why shouldn't He use it when all He was required to do to lay hold of it was to recognize that "I and the Father are one"?

So, dear friend, if you believe in the works of the Father, believe also in His Spirit in the midst of you, waiting to be recognized and put to practical use. Through "Christ in you" you are the "beloved Son" in whom the Father is well pleased.

All power is given unto you in all the affairs of mind and body. Exercise your God-given power, authority, and dominion and rise out of bondage to conditions of lack and discord.

There is a saying that "God helps those who help themselves." You are God's executive, and your indwelling Lord is depending on you to make His glory manifest. Then be up and doing. Do the will of Him who sent you. In so doing you are not only helping yourself but you are helping others.

# Concerning Age

IN THE true thought of life years have no power to take from life that which God has given it. Years have no power to take from life that which God has ordained shall be endless, permanent, enduring, *eternal* life. When we can conceive of life as eternal life, then we shall see that since God is eternal life and has made His Son like Himself, His Son must be given eternal life.

Doesn't Jesus Christ tell us plainly, "He that believeth on the Son hath eternal life?" "I give unto them eternal life; and they shall never perish." "For as the Father hath life in himself, even so gave he to the Son to have life in himself." "I came that they may have life, and may have *it* abundantly."

Jesus Christ resurrected His body temple from the tomb, and He lives in this spiritualized body now, although we cannot see Him with the limited, material vision. He promised that the things He did all His true followers would do.

It is "Christ in you, the hope of glory." Christ is the life principle within each one of us, and we must recognize this to be our ever-increasing life.

You know there is a great deal of overcoming to do that no one can do for us if we expect to inherit this wonderful thing that Jesus intended us to have, eternal life.

We must overcome the bonds that the mortal mind has made for us, and it is not a small matter, we find. As we study the ways of eternal life we put aside all bondage to years and remain in the eternal consciousness of youth of mind and body that God has given us to demonstrate His divine plan.

The race mind introduces into the consciousness the thought of age, unless we rise out of it by an understanding of the unchanging life of Christ within us. The age belief says that at a certain period the body begins to grow a little sluggish, and to take on flesh, and to be less alive. The cell structures respond to this error belief, and the person becomes tired easily, and the body slows down or suffers from pains. All this, you see, is mental. Then there is the physical cause of age. One who does not understand that the body requires certain definite care day by day fails often to do that which is truly best for the body. It is a common error among us that we do not exercise, and rest, and work, and eat, and drink as we should. Food habits are perhaps the most direct in their effects on the system. If you were in a happy state of mind and doing a reasonable amount of work that you love and were eating the foods you should have, your limbs and feet could not trouble you. Swellings and stiffness and soreness are evidence of accumulations in the blood and the tissues. Healing will come through taking the right mental attitude, and getting right down into the body and telling it the Truth; then following up this treatment daily with really sensible and scientific living habits. Supply the foods that are needed, so that the blood stream can be clean and vital and enabled to do its work of washing out the accumulations and rebuilding and perfecting the muscles, and nerves, and bones, and tissues.

\* \* \*

We cannot advise you in the matter of operations; nor do we promise good results from prayer when the individual is deliberately going contrary to the spiritual law of life and health. Youth and the good looks of youth are the fruits of young and eager and joyous and loving attitudes of mind and heart. Obedience to the law of love and life results in harmony and order in the organism. The flesh pictures forth the fixed attitudes of mind.

To resort to patchwork is to get temporary results without changing the cause that produced the imperfection. Rejoice that you have the vision to see the trend of your subconscious mind as pictured forth in your flesh; and pray for more light and for courage to walk in the light.

None of us really likes to see the results of the belief in age, and inharmony, and sorrow, and lack of love, and the sense of human weakness. But it does no good to call them "common" or to seek to patch them up by methods that shock the nerves and make demands upon our resources—without an appreciable improvement in our mental attitude. The only real help is in raising ourselves into the Christ consciousness and permitting this consciousness to work out into all the details of our daily living.

Know that the word of God is in your mouth and in your heart. Rejoice that this is true, and speak the words of Truth with joy, and power, and love. Expect your words spoken and sung to bring results. Weed out all the destructive and negative thoughts and words and tones. Study your voice as an eternal gift of God that has as its source the power and beauty and harmony and substance of God ideas, that responds to your every emotion and thought. Expect it to improve.

Let go of the mental attitude that causes a sense of burden—that belief in age that weights one down with "years." You live in God, not in years; in deeds, not in figures upon a dial. Instead of thinking, "I'm getting up in years," get into the youth spirit of joy in living and loving.

You will notice that we did not say a good "old" man, for you are *not* old. You may have given way to some of the race beliefs in age and failed to take care of yourself and to make full free use of the abundant life and substance of God. But you are really not old.

Now we'll explain. You are a threefold being. No doubt you have learned the facts from your Bible that the Spirit of God dwells in man and gives him breath. And that man has a soul. And a physical body. But have you really studied these facts to understand them, so as to know how to use this threefold nature in the way that God intends?

We have learned and are proving that the very presence and life and intelligence of God are ever abiding in man's being. The Spirit of God is what gives you intelligence and life. Spirit has developed for you that life which we call the soul. And the soul has built the body, and ever continues to renew and rebuild it day by day.

Spirit has no age; it is eternal, as God is

eternal and unchanging. The soul is not old in the sense of its being full of years and decrepitude. The soul is ever unfolding God's ideas, and these are unchangeable. The development of soul qualities causes the individual to be more and more mature in his judgment and his expression, and as the soul is ever keeping in touch with that which is true of God and the Son of God, it is ever refreshed and eager for life's experiences.

The body, which is made up of the action of thoughts of life and love and substance and power and intelligence, in everyone is never old. The very substance that gives the body its form and that nourishes and sustains it is ever new and responsive to the thoughts of life that are impressed upon it.

We are proving that the body is entirely renewed in less than a year, and that one can renew and rebuild it and change its appearance by changing one's thoughts and living habits.

Now, aren't you beginning to take a new interest in life? Won't you stop the next person who says that you are a good "old" man? Let him know that you are being renewed and that God is finding you ready to represent Him in your thoughts and acts.

Physiologists who keep careful watch of the ways of the body now declare that we are renewed bodily in less than a year. Why should flesh age when it is renewed so often?

It must be that the old molds of the mortal mind and the ideas that belong to it need to be remodeled, and the remedy is "Be ye transformed by the renewing of your mind."

Keep on praying for faith, because it is through prayer that you develop all your wonderful qualities of soul. It is not the drugs that do the healing; they are just something tangible upon which to place your attention while God in the midst of you is doing His work of restoration. "I am Jehovah that healeth thee."

So do not think of drugs as being even "props," for they sometimes fill the system with poisons that hinder the healing power of Spirit in its work. If you need something visible to the human eye upon which to place your faith, it might be better to study along the line of dietetics, and give your body the right kinds of food. Right thinking and right eating go hand in hand in keeping one healthy.

The more you think about God's presence of life, purity, love, strength, and health in every fiber of your body temple, the stronger will become your consciousness that your organism is the temple of "Christ in you." God is already in every part of your being, so it is just a matter of being *conscious* of oneness with Him. Your thoughts of Truth form this consciousness.

\* \* \*

We are glad to write your mother, to help her see herself as God sees her and to make use of her God-given power to renew and transform her mind and body through the application of Truth. But we'll not help her to be "old, old, old in years." We'll help her to see that the years only add their wealth of experience and development; that the body never grows old, in fact every cell of the body (if we give it any chance at all) is renewed and replaced in less than a year. So none of us is a year old! The only reason for some folks' seeming to be old, and weak, and inactive is their persistence in thinking the same old thoughts, and getting into ruts, and failing to make use of the good things provided for their needs. Often folks form the habit of taking foods that they do not need and that burden the system year after year. After a time the mechanism that at first handled these food burdens breaks down, and then there are accumulations that begin to hinder perfect circulation and renewal. Then so-called heart trouble, or high blood pressure, or intestinal disorders, may show up. Those who do not understand begin to say, "He is getting old." Not so; he's simply disobeying the health rules!

# *Our Work*

GOD HAS much to be done, and He will reveal the plan to those who seek it, and will open the way of progress and success to those who are really willing to give up preconceived opinions and to grasp the Truth as the Holy Spirit reveals it. Heretofore men have worked for money, labored "for a living." Now men are going to be forced to see that work is for the purpose of expressing God-given faculties and powers and loving service in the way that is truly beneficial. Wasted effort or unwisely directed plans will be a thing of the past. Each thought and each move will be divinely inspired, and results will be satisfying and permanent.

We find that we must be not only good but good for something in this world in which we live. Sometimes we get into a rut and need a change of work, but first we must change our viewpoint.

It surely is not wisdom and good judgment to keep at a thing year after year that brings no appreciable returns and that does not cause the soul to grow and expand and radiate through the body as ever-renewing health and youth. It is foolishness to devote oneself so wholly to a given line of action that one's own consciousness is neglected, so that one fails to learn how to keep in health and strength and how to bring forth the things needed for daily comfort and peace of mind.

The work that God appoints us to never demands of us more than we can do comfortably. And He never obliges us to neglect our own unfoldment of the Christ pattern within us. When we are doing as God would have us do, He takes wonderful care of us, not by bringing supplies and placing them at our feet always, but by showing us how to use our own resources in a way to convert them into whatever we need or would use. One who is living the Christ life attracts blessings of all sorts, and he need never worry about financial matters, though he will give enough thought and attention to them to keep his part of the law.

Many individuals are going through a very definite period of awakening and adjustment these days. And many do not seem to know which way to turn. Employment of the past seems taken away. Nothing that one has done before seems to offer itself. Many times the reason for this is that the soul has been driving itself along certain ruts for a long time, and for its own good needs a change. It is not always best for a person to continue doing that which he likes to do, or that for which he has been trained, or that for which he is paid best. We need to round out, to develop, all our faculties and powers to do that which brings us close to humanity and that which increases what the world needs most. If we do not keep in touch with Spirit and heed its promptings, our own unconscious desires will take us out of the ruts and leave us floundering on the rocks, until we wake up and take hold of something that we shall find we like and that helps us and others.

*　　*　　*

We are declaring and giving thanks each day that Jesus Christ is revealing to each needy one the Truth about supply and the righteous expression of faculties and powers that invites the daily supplies as they are required. It is God's will for all His children to have abundance. And it is our privilege to think this Truth and declare it and expect it to be proved in our life. This is our method of prayer: acknowledging our oneness with God, claiming the ability that this gives, and expecting to have the things needed and conducive to spiritual progress.

We are God's children. But we are also His
brain power, and His hands, and His voice: it
is through us that God expresses His ideas, His
blessings, and brings forth the unmanifest good
in the forms in which we use it. Understanding
this gives one a much better attitude toward
work and makes one confident that one can and
will have plenty to do and will receive compensation for it. As we realize that we are helping God to bring forth His blessings and order,
our work becomes interesting and joy-filled. We
no longer feel that we must overdo in order to
realize as much money as possible. We leave
it to the divine law to bring to us our own; and
we soon see that the better work we do the more
satisfaction and supply we receive, because it
is a law back of the personal relations existing
between men. God never sends a soul into the
world without providing for its needs. Until a
person seeking to find his right work gets the
light and feels the urge to be up and doing, he
is to be still and wait upon the Lord and see His
salvation. Meanwhile instead of worrying about
financial matters and the money to pay expenses,
he should keep going to God and confidently
making known his needs, giving thanks for the
supply. He should give thanks first of all for
wisdom to know what is needed to be done;
then give thanks that the needs are supplied out

of the great storehouse of the Father. He must
bless and break and pass out what he has; and
give thanks and know there is more coming as
he requires it.

*       *       *

There is an inexhaustible supply, and we are
God's beloved children for whom He is ever
providing and to whom He has given His own
life and wisdom and power and substance, the
innate ability to do whatever is required in
bringing our own soul to the Christ standard of
living and serving others.

In order truly to prosper in his work the
individual must keep his mind filled with real
prosperity ideas in right relation. He must think
whether or not he is doing what he really desires to do and must know by divine intuition
that it is helping to develop and to round out
his own consciousness and keep his body strong
and radiant. Also he must understand whether
or not he is serving others to the best of his
ability, and whether he is thinking of them and
feeling toward them that which invites from
them their best and that which is just toward
him. To determine these things requires spiritual discernment and the balanced development
and use of all the faculties of mind. There are
those who arrive at a rather good prosperity

consciousness without being conscious of the
science of Truth. But we find that everyone may
attain his right place if he develops a health and
prosperity consciousness by daily applying himself to the practice of Truth.

\*   \*   \*

This problem of keeping ourselves employed
isn't what it seems. Once we come into the understanding of the true purpose of life and
service, we shall not need to keep busy all the
time doing things we are not particularly interested in, for folks who have no interest in us.
Work has been held up to us, from the time we
were born, as a means of earning a living. We
have been impressed with the thought that we
should be constantly employed and that we
should seek to increase our earning power.

Well, now we are coming to see this matter
in a new light. Work is for self-expression, the
development of God-given faculties and powers, and for helping those about us. Our life and
sustenance are gifts from God and are free—
free for the taking, when we understand how to
proceed of course.

At present we do find it most helpful and
convenient to have some definite arrangement
whereby we serve others and keep the channels
of supply open. As long as we expect to use for

ourselves those things and conveniences which require the efforts of others, we should and must give of our own abilities in some sort of service in return. Many of the most important and necessary things in life are free gifts from God, and we may have them, constantly without any thought of doing any definite thing in return for them. The air we breathe, the sunlight, the beauty of nature, the out of doors for recreation and rest and inspiration. For these we should be thankful to God, and we should be appreciative enough to make the best use of them, that we may the more perfectly interpret His plan in ourselves.

# *Our Methods*

W E ARE glad to have you with us praying for divine guidance, and understanding, and righteousness in all our ways. We do not want anything of the nature of personal ambition to creep into our work or to hinder us in doing that which we feel the Father would have us do. But we cannot always depend on the personal opinions and desires of our students to guide us aright in our handling of the affairs of Unity School. There are matters of universal importance to be considered; and we consider that this body, which has drawn together in a spirit of love and desire to serve, is best able to see and decide and do that which is for the ultimate and highest good of all concerned. Consecration to Truth is one necessary phase of spiritual development. The ability to make practical use of the law is another necessary phase of development. In Bible times Ezra caused his people to repent and turn to God. But he was not the practical businessman and leader who could cause them to go in and rebuild their city, Jerusalem. Nehemiah knew how to direct men, and how to get them to pool and use their funds to best advantage; and he it was who caused the Israelites to rebuild Jerusalem. We are endeavoring, in Unity, to be both consecrated to Truth and practical in our handling of all matters coming to our attention, and in our use of all funds coming to us through love. We are praying daily for guidance, for the truly unselfish use of all that is given. We appreciate the prayers and the cooperation and the letters of counsel that our fellow students offer. And we are willing to have all our efforts that do not measure up to the standard of righteousness fall and come to naught. Sonship in Christ is the goal, and the establishment of the kingdom of heaven in the earth is our aim. If in our immaturity we make mistakes, the law will reveal it, and the love of the Father will forgive (will "give for" the mistakes a better understanding of the things needful) and lead us in a better way. We are not looking for evil or punishment. We are endeavoring to see the Christ in all humanity, and to call attention to and encourage the development of the Christ in all who are receptive. And we are assured that the Christ Mind in us is working in our consciousness to cast out all that does not measure up.

Your frequent crying out in letters for personal help implies lack of faith in God and in us and tends to break up the spiritual conscious-

ness we are helping you to establish. The secret
of our power to help others lies in our refusing
to be moved by the appearances and the apparent lacks that are reported to us, and in our
standing steadfastly holding to the Truth of
being and declaring the working out of the
constructive thoughts and words we have sent
forth, in which we ask those who identify themselves with us to cooperate. No matter what you
tell us of sorrow, or lack, or failure, or illness,
we do not believe it, we do not let it take hold
in our mind and heart. If we should do such a
thing, we should become powerless to help you.
If we should receive and dwell upon all the
troubles that dear ones feel they have and that
they want to impress upon us, we should soon
believe that the world was full of such things
and that God was unable to work out His plan
of life. So we just keep declaring that the things
you write are not true, and we shall continue this
until you too believe them not true and cease
to give your thought to them, and open your
mind and heart and eyes to the glorious Presence
in which you live and which is seeking perfect
expression through you.

*     *     *

We do not promise to say a prayer of words
and have the saying work a miracle in another

individual. Our work is to call attention to the true way of living and to inspire others to want to live in that true way. Our prayers are for the purpose of encouraging those who are making the effort to lay hold of Truth and prove it.

There is much more to living and being healthy than saying one's prayers and reading good books. One must study one's every interest, and inclination, and reaction, and desire in relation to the real Christ wisdom, and love, and power, and life, and substance. The real teacher and healer, then, is the one who not only has faith in God but who understands and makes practical application of the enlightening, and freeing, and healing truths. To heal a man is to free him from the errors that caused his need of healing and to present to him the helpful words and the loving propositions that enable him to be happy and satisfied and eager in applying the Truth as it comes.

\* \* \*

We don't always know just how our efforts at helping others seem until we are in much the same position and are receiving the same consideration and help ourselves! And I suppose it is well that we do have these various vantage points, else how should we ever arrive at the true Christ way of making use of the Father's good and of helping others? We think it quite wonderful to be able to lend a hand financially, or even to restore health. But we shall presently know that the ideal is to radiate such a consciousness of the omnipresence of God that we bring others to a realization of health, and ability, and supply, and the order of the kingdom without anything more from us than our simply *being* the expression of Christ ideas. Then none of us will care to be bothered with more supply than the day calls for. There will be abundance for all. And the individual aim will be for the most worth-while occupation and self-expression!

We're coming to that place swiftly, praise the Light that is for all!

\*   \*   \*

It is my daily joy to bless those who are seeking the way of life more abundant and to offer myself as the hand into which may be placed the message that the heart of the individual is really writing to God.

You remember the spiritual inspiration that Paul had, and this inspiration is also ours as we claim the light and power and love that are God's expression through us:

"If the Spirit of him that raised up Jesus from the dead dwelleth in you, he that raised up Christ Jesus from the dead shall give life also to your mortal bodies through his Spirit that dwelleth in you."

It isn't individuals at Unity who quicken and heal. It isn't the human desire of the individual's own heart that makes the life to flow through his organism more freely. It isn't the thing that we usually think of as Christianity that brings us into the quickening, healing currents of Christ life. It is the stirring in us of the same Spirit of Christ that was and is in Jesus Christ —the Spirit of God—standing forth in the individual as the expression of divine ideas from the mind of Being. It is the soul's willingness and effort actually to live, in daily thinking and acts, the Spirit of Christ, that same Spirit which made Jesus to forget Himself in doing the good and perfect will of His Father. He adored the Father, and sought constantly to glorify Him in making the things of His Spirit manifest in the lives of His children. Jesus was eagerly discovering the real purpose of life and fulfilling it, not for Himself alone but for all of us. He said, "I am the light of the world." "Ye are the light of the world."

\* \* \*

We confer titles on no one, we use no titles ourselves, and we take no account of those which other persons use. We are privileged to use the title "Reverend" if we do desire.

We explain in our literature and from our platform that the real baptism is the baptism of the Holy Spirit. No person or group of persons can give this spiritual baptism—it is a matter between the individual soul and the divine source of all light and life and power and love. When the individual is baptized by the Holy Spirit, that individual knows it, and power from on high is felt and expressed, and is seen by others.

So when you read of those who are using such titles as "Reverend" or "Doctor," or when a center demands such a title of the speaker who is welcomed to its platform, just know that spiritual vision will enable you to look beyond all those outer signs and to discern the real character and ability of the leader or minister.

Our best Unity workers and leaders use no frills. It is their consciousness that draws to them the students they can help, and not their names or the list of books and lessons they have read.

* To those who pass satisfactorily the examinations given on the Unity correspondence course we grant a certificate. Those who complete this course and who prove in other ways that they are capable of ministering from platform, classroom, healing room, and who have

demonstrated that they are trusting to God's divine law of giving and receiving, the law of prosperity, for their success and support—those in whom we have faith and those whom we feel to be loyal Unity workers—may be ordained by us. But after this ordination we expect them to go out and stand on their own feet and build their own work.

Those who know the true purpose of this work are not so much concerned with titles or positions. They are intent upon expressing the Spirit of Christ.

* Editor's Note: The correspondence course is no longer available.

# Transition

W E KNOW that the Truth will open your spiritual eyes and your understanding, and you will know that what seemed to you a loss at the time is no longer to be considered such. You will learn that those who go through the change called death are really passing through a transition, the soul giving up the body temple, which for some reason or other it cannot longer express through or bring into health. Your dear one is not gone away anywhere. He is abiding in the heart of the Father, and you have learned that the Father is omnipresent. And so all His children are just where their own consciousness draws and holds them, whether they are functioning in the physical or have temporarily laid aside the flesh body.

It will help you to know that souls keep on being re-embodied as children until they come into the Christ consciousness and have perfect dominion over mind and body and affairs. Your dear one may already be building a new body temple in which to learn more lessons to unfold the God qualities.

In understanding the law of life and coming into the light of Truth, we give up many of our old conceptions of God and of ourselves and of life here and "hereafter." We find that spiritual unity and love and expression are eternal. And we cease to grieve when a dear one has gone from our sense sight and human surroundings. We enter into the inner place of light and peace, and know that the Father is helping that one to do just what his own soul requires—just as He is ever helping us.

Your hearing your dear one's voice in the night may have been the result of your own subconscious yearning and desire to hear him and to know he was near. Or it may have been his soul's desire and effort to reach your consciousness and comfort you. The soul is consciousness, and those who are spiritually awake can direct their thinking and reach those who are near to them. His thoughts of love could reach you during the stillness of your intellect and your faculties could register the thoughts and report them to the intellect; and you felt that you actually heard the voice. This will make you to know that hearing is mental and that the ears are but instruments to catch and radiate the things heard to the various parts of the body consciousness.

It was not necessary for you to answer. Your dear one felt your response. It is not wise to cling to those who have gone from the body. It tends to bind them to past experiences, and delays possibly their turning to the Father for divine guidance and further progress.

\*　　\*　　\*

Living with memories isn't fulfilling God's plan of your life. God is life, within you, eagerly seeking unity with other life, yearning to picture forth the health and joy and strength and usefulness that there is in all God life. God is love that must be converted into loving—loving things of the present, those about you, the thoughts and words and works that are adding to the wealth and peace and beauty of the world now.

Dear, would it shock you if I told you I do not really believe that those souls whom you have known as friends in the past—and who failed to understand and conform to the divine law of life so that they could stay with the body and work out the divine harmony of His kingdom at the time you knew them in the flesh— are in the least interested in keeping up the old connections and friendships! Why, they are no doubt awake to the fact that they lacked much in the way of light and power and life, and they are surely much more interested in getting at the vital Truth and its application, so that they shall not again fall short and be obliged to change their environment and rebuild a body temple for further expression! These souls who pass through the transition that is termed death are not nearly so likely to crystallize in the past as are some of us who stay on, looking toward the past for our interest and happiness. They must have found it necessary to wake up and get hold of new ideas and make new friendships, to give them inspiration and help.

So bless the past and the old friendships, and turn from them, knowing that they are not the vital issue now. All that another has meant to you has left its imprint upon your soul so that you profit by it daily. And this is all that is of value to you.

There is no reason to suppose that a soul out of the physical body is not aware of what is going on about it. At least, since the soul is consciousness, it is reasonable to assume that it is aware of all that interests it and which it desires to identify itself with.

One who had been spiritually awake and active in soul and body would not be likely to fall asleep even though the body were for some reason given up. Such a one would be on the alert to satisfy his soul hunger and to appreciate all that he could experience without the flesh and the centers of physical structure which his consciousness had built.

It is a sorrow to have a loved one go through the experience of death. But we show a greater love for our dear one by refusing to hang on to the sorrow and by turning the undivided attention to learning how better to live by the divine law, and how to help others to avoid the experience of death. Your son would not have you clinging to him in thought; nor would he wish you to come to him through death. He is a splendid soul, and would have you learn the Truth and live it here and now.

Instead of thinking about going to him, out of the body, begin to be glad that he is coming into the body again, in the splendid way all souls have of getting into the physical—as a babe. The only way by which we shall ever be eternally united with our loved ones is to come into the Jesus Christ consciousness of life. Learn to keep the divine law of life, which means the renewal and transformation of the physical body, so that spirit, soul, and body may remain unified, and the righteous self-expression in all three departments of being may continue.

\*　　\*　　\*

We are with you constantly, dear, to help you to realize that all is well. Your dear one did not know how to let go of the limitations into which her mind had got, nor how to renew and build up her body. And so to her it is a rest, and an opportunity, to lay aside the body for a time and to break the conscious connection with things going on around her, until the divine urge within her again prompts her to build the body temple and take up lessons here in the physical.

If your mother had gone away on a vacation and you knew she was in loving hands, you would not be grieved or worried, would you? Well, now, that is just what has taken place. She is resting from the suffering and the problems that she did not know how to manage. She is in the presence of God, just as you are; and the best way to show your love for her is just to let go of all human longing and all sense of loss, so that this soul who welcomed you as a babe. and who has cared for you, may rest assured all is well with you. For your mother has just gone into a different schoolroom of life, where the divine Father-Mother is the teacher.

# Maternity

TRULY it is a blessed privilege to prepare for the coming into the physical of a soul, who is coming to dwell among us to unfold more of the consciousness of sonship. And the parents who invite a soul in this realization, and who consecrate themselves to doing their utmost to keep in health and to provide an atmosphere of peace and joy and purity and prosperity, are really blessed and initiated into something very like heaven.

There is so much that is holy and sweet and helpful in getting ready for a baby. There is a communion of soul that lifts one up and brings one out in new ways and holds one to one's best.

You will find this experience invaluable in helping your other children to see the reality of life, and to learn to express love and unselfishness. It will be quite the most wonderful thing for them to hear from you that you are to have a wee baby to love and to care for and to train! Let them feel a personal interest in the baby's coming and in all the preparations for it. It will be a splendid time to give them needed lessons in physiology, and the care of the body, and the relations of men and women.

\* \* \*

Let your soul magnify the Lord, as did the mother of Jesus. There is but one presence and one power, God, the good. He is the Father of all, and since you are full of faith and are looking to Him for help in every need, He is preparing the way for your child to come forth easily, joyously, in perfect safety. His love surrounds, enfolds, and protects you, and all is well.

Relax and free every muscle in your body from tenseness. Underneath are the everlasting arms to uphold, to strengthen, and to sustain you, so you can relax and rest in the assurance that you are being protected, that you are being strengthened, and that the way is being made easy for a safe confinement.

The vitalizing life of the Spirit fills you to overflowing with all the strength, vigor and vitality you need to sustain you. In His presence is fullness of joy.

In "your oneness with God everything is now and will be in divine order," and all is well.

\* \* \*

You and the wee one beneath your heart are very near and dear to the great heart of the

Father, and since you are looking to Him in prayer and in faith, you have opened the way for your babe to come into God's beautiful world in a harmonious way.

God is the Father of your child, you know, so you can trust Him to take care of His own and to prepare the way for it to enter the world in perfect safety for you and your babe as well.

Let your soul magnify the Lord as Mary the mother of Jesus did, and let your soul rejoice in God your Saviour.

"God is love," and divine love harmonizes, strengthens, enfolds, heals, and protects you. God in the midst of you is a tower of strength and stability. God is the health of His people, and He is your strength and health.

\*     \*     \*

Let your heart rejoice that the divine Father-Mother is giving into your keeping one of His little ones, whom you may pour out your love on, and wisely direct and encourage in the development of all the faculties and talents that each soul has and is eager to use. Praise your splendid body for its marvelous construction and its perfect work in lending itself to the needs of this other soul just now. Know that the Creator who has planned such a mind and body is ever working to carry out His creation.

For every soul coming into the physical the Father-Mother makes ample provision of everything required. This gives joyous assurance that all is well and that another member in the family will bring his own prosperity with him. Divine love will find ways in which to increase the earning capacity, the inflow of supply, the happiness in using what comes. Divine wisdom will direct, so that all things will work together for good to all.

So instead of thinking of the babe who is on the way as an additional expense, think of him as a blessing, and a bringer of prosperity. Instead of thinking of the days of constant care, think of the joyous lessons he is going to teach, and of the individual contributions to the family's happiness. Each soul that is welcomed into the world brings its own individual blessings and gifts to the world!

\*     \*     \*

The stomach, or that part of the solar plexus directly connected with the stomach, is the substance center, and it is here that the mental faculty of judgment finds its center of action. Directly below the substance center, at the navel, is the center of order. Thoughts and feelings and habits that have to do with keeping one's mind and body and affairs in order register here at the lower part of the solar plexus and the navel.

The perfect order of the law of life is established in you through your permitting the creative ideas of life and love and substance and intelligence to direct your thoughts and the functions of your body. The omnipresent substance of God is appropriated and impressed with the perfect patterns (for your own sustenance and for the formation and sustenance of the new body temple for the soul who is coming to dwell with you), as you keep mind and heart confident that God is taking care of you and yours and that Spirit knows how to arrange for the manifestations through you of that which is best, and for the inflow from any source of all things needful.

We are declaring that the Holy Spirit overshadowing you, working in you, now frees you from all the impressions of past experience, and gives you a new understanding of life and substance, and establishes in you a new order, quickens a new judgment, floods you with a new light that directs you in ways of peace and health and happiness.

This dear little babe is bringing everything it will require with it from the Father's great store. The manifestations will come as there is need, and as you and the dear daddy, and all

whom the Father may direct, are true to what He
would have you do and to the light of spiritual
understanding and loving service.

Parents are but representing the divine Father-Mother in receiving and caring for these
new temples that souls are building for experience and further development of their God-
given faculties and powers. Remembering this
takes away the sense of anxiety and burden and
gives a great peace and joy and consciousness of
power and love and prosperity.

\*　\*　\*

When negative attitudes of mind and heart
cause depression and physical inharmony and a
feeling of lack and worry, a quiet hour for a
real study and prayer will flood your soul with
an entirely new light and peace. And you will
begin to relax, and to allow the abundant life
and the wonderful love of God to flow freely
through you, restoring order and health. You
will also see your affairs in a different light, and
the inner assurance that God is providing, and
directing, and prompting will give you great
peace. You also will invite and lay hold of your
own individual God-given resources. For in
truth God does provide for you, and your blessings are not dependent upon others. You can
use your own faculties and powers, and bring

forth that which you require—and you will be the better for this purposeful living.

Just now, especially, you do not want to worry or be anxious for the future. You want your mind and your body calm and peaceful and happy, so that you will be radiating only the best and most helpful things to your unborn babe. Your own attitude is imparting qualities to the soul of your child.

So just make up your mind that you are going to live in a little world all your own, a world of beauty, and peace, and happiness, and health, and simple pleasures. To think lack, or possible failure, or that one's close companion may not do the part he should in a splendid way, is to send irritating currents over the nerves, and to use up one's store of energy, and to impress the ever-present substance of God with the appearance of lack and inharmony. You do not want this. You want the effect produced by faith in God. Have your communion and identification with the divine Father-Mother elements of being. For, truly, you are representing God, the Father-Mother, in preparing to nurture and receive and help this soul which is embodying through you. And God is giving you the needed wisdom and poise and love and sustenance to meet all the requirements. Your part is to believe this, and to trust, and keep busy with the things that are yours to do, without anxiety or concern about what others are doing. Trust God to prompt others to do their part. Praise the God qualities in your husband; expect him to express them in practical ways.

There is great responsibility, yes. But there is great satisfaction in determining to meet it, to be fair to the soul you have invited, to make a home in which that soul may develop its spiritual powers as well as its physical temple. Not a great deal of money is required. The thing that counts is that the money comes through your own and your husband's own eager efforts.

Social position means nothing to the incoming soul—all the traditions to the contrary notwithstanding. What the soul asks is opportunity to be itself. Happy, peaceful, truly wise and practical parental companionship means everything. And you can have this to offer your child if you will to do it.

# To Truth Teachers

JESUS SAID, "I chose you, and appointed you, that ye should go and bear fruit, and *that* your fruit should abide: that whatsoever ye shall ask of the Father in my name, he may give it you."

When we expect God's help in our expression and prosperity, we are to come in the name of sons—in the consciousness of sonship. We are to see to it that the work we are doing is the Father's work and the very highest type of real service of which we feel capable. When we know this to be true, we are not anxious or concerned with results. We are interested in carrying out the Father's directions and in doing that which is truly best for all concerned.

We can of course throw ourselves, our God-given faculties and powers, into personal efforts, and accomplish given and desired results. But unless we are truly working in perfect tune with the Infinite and doing that which is our present best and that which best meets the highest needs of our own soul we shall not be wholly satisfied even though we gain that which we set out to attain.

Remember we are to pray in the name of

Jesus Christ, which means with the same earnest desire to glorify God in our life that filled Jesus' mind and heart always. We are to ask of the Father in the realization of our oneness with Him and the consciousness of sonship.

Jesus says that if we love Him, we will keep His commandments. Remember what those commandments are? "Thou shalt love the Lord thy God with all thy heart, and with all thy soul, and with all thy strength, and with all thy mind, and thy neighbor as thyself."

It is the Lord God within us that we are to be devoted to—to love, unify ourselves with, be obedient to. Our own spiritual self must have our attention and love and care and consideration. If we are neglecting our own spiritual development, our own health, we are not keeping this first and greatest commandment. And if we are not keeping it, we cannot keep the second.

So before we can truly pray, as Jesus says we should, and in answer to which He says the Father will do what we ask Him, we must learn really to love our own spiritual self and to do that which is best for us—and incidentally best for all others.

When heart and mind and body are filled with the consciousness of the love of God and fellow men, we are prospering. That which we are prompted to do is accomplished. We are

fearless and happy because we know that we
are doing our part to establish and maintain
God's kingdom in the earth.

* * *

While you are more in the realm of the soul,
where the activity of the psychic forces im-
presses you with the negative phases of humanity's development, you will feel the weight of
human woe and will tend to grieve and worry
and resent that which seems unfair and unjust
and cruel. But as you raise yourself into the
Christ consciousness and see as God sees, you
will look through and beyond appearances and
begin to understand the true state of affairs and
to discern just what is taking place in men. You
will be just as diligent in helping people, but
you will no longer give way to seeing greed and
the crushing of some men by others, injustice;
but you will understand that what is taking
place is a process of growth, and you will bless
this growth and see man becoming more and
more Christlike.

It may be, blessed friend, that you have been
overtaxing that body of yours by giving forth
more than you have taken the time and quiet-
ness to receive. That physical man in us is a
willing and obedient servant and does what we
tell him to do, but we mustn't be a heavy task-

master and try to drive him beyond what he has developed the capacity to endure. In my very own experience I find that it is always best to listen and obey when I receive the hint to take things easier. At times when I've disregarded the hint, I've received the kick also.

Remember that your heart is and always will be right with God. It is the throne of love, and "God is love." You are eternally one with your source and Creator, so it's just a matter of getting still, peaceful, calm, and serene, with your thought away for a while from all the outer activities, and opening the way for the mighty and abundant inflow of Spirit that vitalizes, invigorates, builds up, and renews every "place" in mind, heart, soul, and body.

Your Creator is always on the job, and through our united prayers Christ the living Word is bringing into manifestation what is already an established part of your being—wholeness.

Unlimited as the infinite Provider is as our resource, we must still the restless mortal in order to receive; then deep and full shall the inner breath be to fill our relaxed and receptive organism. You are rested now and there is no compelling force to urge you to outer action. "He sent forth his word and healed them." Bless you!

\*     \*     \*

Perhaps you did not make the complete connection when you started the new work and that was why the body did not seem to stand up to the work you needed to accomplish. We have to make our whole connection, spirit, soul, body, the wholeness—the holiness is in getting them all together—all working in harmony. But we are forgetting this and seeing you connected up all the way through and one with the all-supplying stream of life and substance and power and love and light. We have to lay hold of this concept of God as eternal, as active eternal Principle, all-supplying substance, not as something that comes and goes and gives out. The things we observe all give out, but we have to get back of this to the abiding consciousness of Jesus Christ—the same yesterday, today, and forevermore. And what does that mean? God's supply is always the same. And when a son of God appropriates and uses God, why, he becomes all that the Father planned and does all that the Father wills.

Now, my dear you are taking this all-supplying substance for yourself. I see you capable of going on with strength, wisdom, power, and joy. I witness your soul satisfied and blessed in God. The waters of life are ever flowing from the throne of God in your heart, the place of authority from which you send forth your mandates.

I am finding myself that if I want to keep the outer organization, I have to be appropriating and transmuting the coarser.

We must know the chemistry of the body; we must find the whole man. We have need of this outer man and we have to make the mortar that builds him up to a full development.

Dear heart, you and I both realize that the supply is in the One, that the One never runs short of supply. Now when we get the concept of this and it becomes a habit for us to appropriate and apply this consciousness as we do the air that is constantly ready for our use, we shall be one with the omnipresent reservoir of God supply and have no more lack of any kind.

\* \* \*

God in the midst of you is a tower of strength and stability. You are filled with the vim, vigor, vitality, and tireless energy of "Christ in you," and you are renewed every moment of the day.

It may be, dear friend, that you have been trying too hard in a personal way and have not taken time to relax, to let go, and realize that "I am in the Father, and the Father in me."

Sometimes our attention becomes so engrossed
in the things we are trying to do that we forget
to unify ourselves consciously with the source
of our being.

You are the executive of your indwelling
Lord, and every instant you draw from Him the
wisdom, life, energy, strength, power, and substance to meet the moment's most pressing need;
as your consciousness becomes one with His,
you realize that it is not by personal might, nor
by personal power, but by the Spirit of the Lord
that all things are accomplished.

When you pray for another, your word of
Truth quickens, awakens, and stirs to action
the Spirit within that individual, so you do not
need to lose any of your vital force when you
realize that the word does the work. In this realization your patients do not draw upon your
energy.

You are developing your inner resources of
Spirit, and becoming more alive through the
resurrection of new powers from day to day.
The powers you are unfolding are your assurance of prosperity and success in the outer, for
demonstrations of life and prosperity go hand
in hand.

I am joining you in the Godward thought,
and the thanksgiving that there is only one
Presence and one Power in you and through

you, and present at your meeting Sunday evening. Keep it constantly in your mind that you as a limited entity are not there visible to the eager crowd; but that God is there expressing divine ideas, manifesting His blessings, through His own image-likeness children. Instead of looking out and seeing the sense evidences, or listening to the complaints or the woes or the trials of those gathered to witness the Truth, look directly and with undivided attention to God, the good.

\* \* \*

Now, I know just how you feel about wanting to walk with me, to take my hand, to be held close in the embrace that gives peace and courage, to join in song of rejoicing for the unlimited good. But that feeling isn't all what it seems! It isn't me that you want to be closer to; it is your own Lord: you want to be consciously one with what to you represents an advance over what you have yet realized! And the longing is the prayer of your heart that brings fulfillment! Isn't that glorious?

You are too much inclined to the mental, as it is. The depletion you experience when you talk to others, or when you help them, is due to your mental sensitiveness—your ability to sense needs, and to supply mentally, out of your own great store, that which the others lacks. But you must rise out of this phase of development, out of this means of helping others. The Jesus Christ consciousness of life gives you the spiritual poise and ability to see beyond the seeming conditions through which others are passing. It gives you power to stir up in them and to call into expression their God-given abilities to meet their own needs.

Jesus Christ sees as God sees. He sees the perfection of man; He holds us in our perfection. His holding us there and drawing us up into the perfection of Himself does not in any way deplete His own consciousness or tear down His own body. There was a time in His unfoldment when Jesus did experience such mental activity and such depletion. At such times He withdrew from the multitudes for a while, to get back into His consciousness of oneness with God and the universal and inexhaustible resources of Spirit. When He healed the woman who had an issue of blood, He was conscious that virtue had gone out from Him because the woman had come to Him and touched Him, to get the personal help. You see, His consciousness of life and love reached out into His garments; and He was conscious of that which touched even His clothing. Later He had risen out of that particular state in which

He felt virtue leaving His body to merge with the body of another; and had established Himself in the spiritual realm where His consciousness of life and substance merges with the entire race consciousness, and where we may all come in touch with Him and receive the spiritual help without depleting Him. He has learned to appropriate more but to refrain from drawing boundary lines. The human believes in limitations and fixes the inflow and outflow of life. We rise out of these limitations and boundaries by degrees. As we learn how to use these qualities and powers in divinely ordered ways, we are ready to let down the walls of separation, which at one time were protections.

As you learn to see the fullness of God's life and love and power and substance in others, you will know that you need not pour out your own for them. You will have the knowledge and the light to call their attention to what they have and to prompt them to use it.

You ask, "What's wrong with me?" My dear, we are not looking for the "wrong" things; with our spiritual eye of faith that beholds only the divine image and likeness, we are seeing you as the Father created you in the beginning—whole, illumined, full of faith, perfect. By seeing you from God's standpoint we help you to manifest your innate divinity.

Take your own eyes away from appearances as they seem to the limited, human vision. Be diligent in holding to your innate Christ perfection under all circumstances.

The word of Truth is the power that does the work effectively, and when you use the word instead of your own vital force, when you wish to help others, there will be no aftereffects in your own mind or body. When you practice the laying on of hands you weaken your own powers of resistance and easily take on the condition you wish to dissolve in your patient.

It is a limitation to try to use your personal power in healing others. Constantly keep in mind the truth that *it is not I, but the Father within me, He doeth the works.* Say with Jesus, "The Father abiding in me doeth his works."

It is necessary for the healer to establish himself in the consciousness that perfection is the only reality; there is only one Presence and one Power in the universe, God, the good omnipotent.

Deny the belief, the appearance, of disease (or discord of any kind) and realize that it is *nothing.* Think of it as dissolved into nothingness, and with your eye of faith see the Christ perfection established in the place that needs to manifest the reality of good.

Conserve your vital force and your thought

force. Then your whole being will be strengthened, and you will become too positive to take on any false belief. Your thoughts of Truth tend to make you positive.

When you speak the word to help others, know that it is "Not by might, nor by power, but by my Spirit, saith Jehovah of hosts." The word quickens the Spirit in your patients to action, and the Spirit in them "doeth his works." God in the midst of you ministers unto them and calls forth the divinity they need to express.

\* \* \*

It is possible, you know, to drive oneself beyond what the soul and body can stand up under, if wisdom and love do not prompt. One may lean too much toward intellectual activities —drawing and holding too much of the blood and nerve energy in the upper part of the body, and causing congestion and depletion. One may devote oneself so wholly to those things, good in themselves, which require undivided attention and nerve strain that the playtimes for the body (not the usual social activities, which do not really permit the body to relax and renew itself while the mind is engaged in dwelling upon the purely natural things of life) are neglected. So we try to encourage our folks to seek to live balanced lives, being fair to the body, regardless of the soul's eager pace to keep up with the things that it considers most vital.

One could engage in so-called spiritual work to the point of losing one's health. In order to benefit humanity most we must each one see to it that we are fair to ourselves and that we live a life that increases our power and strength and health.

"What doth it profit a man, to gain the whole world, and forfeit his life?" We might gain many persons and bring them to our spiritual convictions, yet if we lost our own health and consequently our life, our work would not be pleasing in God's sight. For God is the very mind and life within us that is seeking to blend and coordinate the faculties of mind and express them in the substance that we term the manifest life.

\*     \*     \*

There is no limit to the so-called "miracles" that can be performed by those who consecrate themselves wholly to do the will and the work of Christ.

"Where two or three are gathered together in my name, there am I in the midst of them."

We know that as you continue to hold fast to the living Christ, you and all your blessed coworkers will be illumined and prospered in ever-increasing measure.

The blessings that you have already received are only the beginning of a glorious outpouring and spiritual growth that will continue always.

\*    \*    \*

"God shall supply every need of yours according to his riches." This is the greatest promissory note ever written, and it is one that you can cash every hour of every day at God's ever-present "bank" and storehouse of supply.

The wonderful energies of Spirit that restore you to wholeness are there waiting for you to express them along lines of profitable service to God and humanity.

As you help others spiritually and in every way you not only fulfill the law of giving and receiving, but you develop your own resources and capabilities in fuller measure. By helping others under the guidance of the Spirit of truth you at the same time help yourself. So do not let the limited concepts of others interfere with your giving loving service. You are right in maintaining that you can help others demonstrate "higher" than you yourself have demonstrated, because it is not through personal might, nor personal power, but it is by the Spirit of the Lord that all things are accomplished. "The Father abiding in me doeth his works." God is

the one and only Helper in the universe, and all
the good we ever enjoy is brought forth through
His power.

*     *     *

But, dear, I am inclined to feel that we all
must arrive at the place where we do as Jesus
did when He saw that so many demands were
being made upon Him for help that He could
not give Himself fully enough to what the
Father was directing Him to do. He asked
Spirit to show Him men in whom dwelt the
qualities that could be developed to make them
successful healers and teachers and leaders.
Then, whether there was anything in the life or
attitude of the prospective worker to indicate
his readiness or even his willingness to change
his occupation or to take up spiritual training,
Jesus approached him and spoke of His conviction and asked the man to follow Him. He
didn't seem to have much difficulty in getting
a group of men to drop what they were engaged
in to take up with eagerness and devotion and
diligence the things He considered necessary
to success in spiritual service.

You are "unspeakably busy" doing the
things that come to you for attention, and really
don't have time for the things that would make
you a greater and more powerful leader. There

are others in your city who have not enough to do to encourage their own development. I know you have tried to get helpers in your center, and you have no doubt approached all who seemed to possess the desired qualifications.

But it must be that there are those who would love to help and who would be blessed in such work. Let us unite in prayer for your discernment, discrimination, and authority to look for and to select those in whom some particular spiritual quality are dominant and ready for practical training.

\* \* \*

You speak of the comfort and soul food you enjoyed during your hours with me. That is splendid temporarily. But, dear, if you were with me daily, I might at any time do something that would hurt you just as badly as some of the things others have done have hurt. Personalities, as such, do not have the capacity for always satisfying one another. And the persons who are still depending on outer expressions of love and consideration are likely to be disappointed or disillusioned at any moment. For truly there just isn't real joy and light and power and substance in the things of the senses, or always in the relations of those who are seeking to let Christ ideas prompt them in their in-

dividual expression. Our real source of help
in every need is the Holy Spirit within; and as
we keep poised in Spirit, we find ways to reach
others in Spirit and call out the best in them
and to understand them in a wonderful new
way.

If you truly feel that the Jesus Christ Spirit is
inspiring you and giving you power to teach
and heal and prosper, I am sure that you will
find plenty to do. What I can't understand is
that, assuming you were being divinely
prompted, you seemed to feel that you must go
and sit there at that center, under the direction
of others and limited apparently by their decisions. If there were things that the Father
would have had you do, why didn't you go
about doing them—without regard to what
others were doing? And if your attention had
been directed Godward, you surely would have
been so occupied with splendid constructive
thoughts and work that you wouldn't even have
noticed what the others were doing. You were
bound in personal consciousness and sensitiveness (subconsciously perhaps), and this made
you feel disturbed at what you believed the
others' attitude toward you to be. With your
mind cluttered up with conflicting beliefs and
feelings, you were not in shape to handle the
work the Father would have brought to you.

Remember and be encouraged, dear, that when we began to awaken and to feel the urge to minister, there was no such thing as a Unity center, not even friends who saw things as we did. We did come in touch with a few, and were together in a class. But we all had to branch out and start using what we got in our own way, meeting whatever need presented itself. It was the thing that shone in our face and the results we got through our prayers that drew others to us. And we hadn't time to think much about what success we were having, there was so much to be done for the family, and our own eager study of whatever words of Truth we could find or hear kept us busy. We were not thinking of the approval of others or how they regarded us. And not depending on any gathering or other folks' cooperation, we were perfectly free to do whatever work the Father brought. We didn't ask for work; it just came right to our home. Someone would hear through another that we had something good and would come.

Turn away from all these conflicting and confusing and discouraging thoughts and appearances, and give your interest and undivided attention to God. You remember little Samuel, don't you? He had gone into the temple, and was ever hovering about to do whatever might be given him to do. And one night he was aroused and thought he heard Eli, the priest, calling him. He ran to Eli, but discovered that Eli hadn't called him, and became quiet again. Again he heard the voice; and Eli then explained to him that it might be Jehovah, and told him to speak to Jehovah—and the revelation of Spirit came. Read the account in I Samuel, the third chapter. You will notice that there is special mention of "both the ears" of everyone that hears the doing of Jehovah! Let us consider your problem in the light of little Samuel's experience. You have given yourself to service at the temple. You have been responding to the dictation of others. At last there is evidence that the Lord is endeavoring to speak to you. You don't get the message by going first to one and then to another of your associates, or even by coming to us. You must talk with Jehovah (your own Lord God, in the midst of you). And when you know what it is Jehovah is saying to you, don't be afraid to do it! Samuel heard things that seemed to be uncomplimentary to the priest Eli and his sons, and he feared to tell them. But Eli came to Samuel to know what had been prophesied. Eli was a priest and supposedly the law giver, but prejudice and ambition came in and interfered with his service. But even in the midst of this there was Samuel (which means "name of God"), bringing the soul into conscious communion with God so that the spiritual prophecy might be given and the way of deliverance from further bondage made clear.

When we do our best and continue to look to God for our light, and ability, and opportunities for expression and service, the divine law works out our problems and we have more grace and glory than we had anticipated.

Those who meet the public are supposed to be poised and well rounded in their spiritual development, and so filled with love and joy and health and consciousness of supply that they fairly radiate it to all who come near— not starved for kindness and understanding and love and encouragement! Those who need help themselves don't belong in the work where they are continually faced with the problems of others. They should get into something that they have wanted to do and that will tend to unfold their own faculties and powers in such a way as to prove that they are ready for the larger field of service. So long as you are so disturbed by what others do or fail to do, you are hardly abiding in the Christ consciousness, from which you should work in the spiritual ministry.

\* \* \*

No, there is no lack of cooperation among

students so long as they keep in the Truth consciousness. But the adverse beliefs of the ages will come up to be handled. The closer we are associated the more we invite from one another the shortcomings that exist in us and that must be brought to the surface, recognized, and made to measure up to the Christ standard. The advantage of groups of Truth students being so closely associated is that they form the habit of constantly reminding one another of the unfailing law and unchanging Principle. Truth students who are loyal to Christ are not given to smoothing things over, or making excuses for the error beliefs or the cries of the human self as it must relinquish its prejudices. In Christ we learn to brace ourselves for the shocks that the uprooting process sometimes causes, if not really to welcome the experiences that show us how we stand. We learn to be less concerned with what others are doing and more concerned with our own attitude toward their doings. We are less eager to impress folks and more determined to have something worth their heeding before we offer it. We are willing to still the eager but often mistaken intellectual offerings, that the Christ word may fill our heart and quicken our senses and establish its order in the earth.

Dear one, you are becoming consciously established in the poise of the Christ Mind,

where you are constantly open and receptive
to new ideas, new inspiration, new vitality.
Spirit always comes forth to meet the needs,
whatever they may be. You are putting the personal self aside in order that the capacity of the
Christ I AM may be demonstrated.

You are growing so at one with universal
Mind that you speak from the consciousness of
your divine self, which knows intuitively what
to say to help each one of those dear seekers
after Truth who comes to you for aid in reading
the divine law. In the one all-knowing Mind we
all live, move, and have our being. You are
open, receptive, and obedient to the inner leading, and thus are a free avenue through which
the Father reaches His children with His message of Truth.

We all of us "with unveiled face beholding
as in a mirror the glory of the Lord, are transformed into the same image from glory to
glory." My! how radiant and beautiful we are
all becoming!

The success of teachers and healers and
leaders lies in their being able and willing to
bear witness to the Christ ideas active in the
consciousness of those whom the Father draws
to them, and not in their telling what they per-
sonally can do or have done. All of us more or
less give way to this habit of introducing per-

sonal ways and opinions and desires into our work. We are praying and knowing that all that does not measure up to the Christ method of living and teaching is falling away from us, that we may do the perfect will of the Father.

# To Married People

IT IS truly wonderful to have children and to be truly awake in caring for them, that they may grow up in health and poise and the assurance that they are God's and that all things needful come through them and to them.

The first five to six years of an individual's life are very important, and to keep him healthy and happy and busy with suitable entertainment and work during that period means everything. He is truly laying his foundation and preparing his many faculties for other activities that are to follow.

Grownups and their children can do without homes of their own, without good furniture, without cars, without many of the luxuries that have grown to be everyday habits with many. But all of them, large or small, need time for quiet and for well-planned meals and for attention to the little things (little in themselves, but necessary to health). Daily study with Unity helps to gain the understanding and faith that make these things possible.

\* \* \*

Some way you have come to believe that a constant repetition of words representing Truth is necessary in order to live as you should and to establish order in your affairs. In reality, the repetition of words, however true they are, cannot make things right if they are not right at the foundation. For example, you used to keep blessing and praising your husband and declaring guidance and prosperity for him. But he wasn't cooperating, and so there was only a condition of cross-currents and a delusion of the personality resulting from personal assurances, without the inner confirmation of Spirit and without the purposeful cooperation of all the faculties and powers in living the Christ life. And since, you have been thinking so constantly of your children, and doing more than they themselves are doing to try to bring them into the Truth way of living. Now, the most helpful thing is just to give them actual freedom. Stop thinking of their problems; leave them to their own resources, and let them feel the need for spiritual quickening and Truth for themselves.

If it helps you to study and pray constantly, do it. But try to grasp the full value of each and every word, speak it deliberately and with assurance, and then let it rest in the soil of your mind and in the elements of being from which it is to form blessings, until it brings results.

Don't keep repeating the word, assuming that it hasn't yet taken root.

\*     \*     \*

Certainly you don't need to bother with the child's speech! Or with the tendency you call "stubbornness"! Why, dear, he has a right to be "stubborn" if others keep at him too persistently! He must release his own powers and be permitted to try them out unprompted much of the time. Too much attention and help and fretting, even silently, on the part of parents is responsible for the "I can't" habit. Suppose he doesn't do a thing as well as you could do it. That is no reason for your correcting him or showing him how to do it—let him do it his way and discover later, by himself, that he can do better and better, until he perfects his expression. He will have much more interest in trying things, if you permit him more freedom in doing them alone. To take away that "stubbornness" would spoil a wonderful God quality in the early stages of development, and he would have to work hard for years, later on in life, to regain the proper use of it. So don't try too hard to make your child just what you feel he should be. Let God in the midst of him interpret for him and bring forth His conception of this particular child of His. God knows best.

\*    \*    \*

You feel that you and your wife have not done your full parental duty. Well, who of us can say that he has? For that matter, we are all children, floundering in our immaturity, making mistakes, learning to love and forgive, looking to the Father-Mother of us all for light and strength and training!

Let's not condemn ourselves or resent it if at times a dear one feels a spurt of ambition or anxiety, or fails to see things just as we do. Let's endeavor to look through the veil of personality and see the Christ within, and trust this God self to come through, gloriously!

I want to add something to what you said of the past and the future. The "past is what it is," but we do not often understand it and see it as it really is. The past recedes from us if we do not hug it to us, and the light that the changing perspective throws upon it makes it a pleasing background for present activities! As we rise higher in consciousness, the whole is revealed as a wondrous picture of the soul's progress.

The future is what we make it. But we are learning that we are developing God-given faculties and powers, coming into consciousness of sonship. So after all the future is in God's hands, and it will reveal in our life the state that Jesus called the kingdom of God or the kingdom of the heavens. The order of the universe established in man's daily life!

*       *       *

Let's remember that those children are God's children. You know this in theory, but in actual fact do you think of them hour by hour as the Father's children, unfolding out of His life and love and wisdom and provided for out of His inexhaustible store? Are you teaching them that they are God's children, that He is the Father, and that they must look to Him by turning their thoughts to their own capacity to interpret the divine plan and to do that which opens the way of supply to them? Or are they growing up looking to you for what they want and need, depending on you to think out the problems and to bring forth the good things?

Not all their education is coming through the schools, you know! It is your privilege and duty to give them the Truth of their being, and to see to it that they enter into the consciousness of Truth and make practical use of it in all their ways. Otherwise you push them forward intellectually, without the proper spiritual development and daily use of their faculties in meeting what life brings their way.

You are no doubt too anxious about the

children and their schooling. You must keep remembering that their education is from within out. The outer opportunities come as their inner development requires them, and it is all a matter of God-Mind unfolding and bringing about that which is best for all concerned. When you become personal and anxious, you push and cause tension. The children may cram what is offered them, but will they be really eagerly assimilating and making use of what comes? Let them hunger for opportunities and they will open the way for their own progress.

\*    \*    \*

Sometimes the very efforts of a wife and mother to go beyond the home to bring in supply and to establish the social life on a higher level through such efforts, will tend to depress and discourage and to lessen the initiative and executive ability of the husband and father. Wives usually help best by standing back of the husband, and inspiring him with the feeling that his ideas are good, his undertakings worth while, the results satisfying, even though they themselves feel confident they could do better! Occasionally we find that a splendid wife will use her ideas, without realizing it, in the effort to inspire and push the husband into doing that which she feels he should and could do. Not having come from his own inspiration and ability, the plan falls flat or fails to bring the splendid results dreamed of.

We need to remember that work and business are, after all, just means of developing certain soul qualities and avenues through which we serve others in return for the services rendered us. That which the soul really desires to do is its present way of progress and success. To clear away the feeling that one must do what others expect of one, or do what seems to promise larger returns because of obligation, is the greatest help another can give.

The real life of the home, the intercourse of members of the family, the development of each soul, means so much more than does the kind of house you live in, the things worn, the neighbors you associate with, the things purchased or used which the bills represent. I am sure you know this, but the constant suggestions on every hand of the desirability of things tends to pull one away off center—until one forms the daily habit of keeping in close touch with Spirit.

\*　　\*　　\*

Now, dear, just turn your entire attention to God and earnestly seek to see as He sees. See your children as eagerly growing souls. See them as individuals unfolding their own facul-

ties and powers, individually doing that which
seems to them best at the moment. Let your
mind rise to the heights where you can view life
on a larger scale. See these souls not bound by
conventional millstones and others' opinions
and their own immediate personal problems,
but as sons of God learning by experience and
by yearning and by inspiration the way of Truth
in life. Forget the present in the eternal; rejoice
that all God's children are coming to know His
plan of life. Be not only willing but happy to
think of your children and all others as they
are in God's kingdom—free, free to live life as
they see it. Free to change, where they feel
they have made mistakes, or where the present
mode of living seems to depress or to hinder
progress. Free to stand for their highest ideals,
assured of blessings from others.

\*     \*     \*

I feel that I know how you must think and
feel in this matter of your children; for you are
looking on with the eyes of a devoted mother
and feeling with the heart that knows sacrifice
and loyalty and righteous ambition. But really
in handling such a "problem" (this word does
not describe just what is meant) one must have
more of the positive ability of the masculine
soul and less of the negative or feeling side of

the feminine soul. You, as other women are wont to do, are *feeling* much more than you are *thinking*. The feeling is human and based on personal views and past experience. So it will not serve as a power in solving the problem; it will throw in a disturbing element and tend to confuse. But if you will turn your attention to really *thinking* about this matter in the splendid way a man will think out the best method of procedure, you will open your mind and heart to the Christ ideas. Then you will begin to be a real help, for you will release these children from preconceived opinions as to the suitable thing to do.

In His sight your child is perfect. The standards of weight, height, and so forth that man has set up as a guide are not by any means in accord with God's idea of what is good and perfect. So don't worry or be in the least anxious about the weight of your little one. What is really important is the "stature" of her "inward man," her soul and consciousness. To measure up to the Jesus Christ standard she must keep her thoughts good, pure, lovely, joyous, beautiful, and based on the Truth.

When she does this, her body temple is bound to show forth the perfection of the Christ within.

\*    \*    \*

We are lifting you up in the great love and light that will make you feel the peace of Jesus Christ and rest in the assurance that all is well. Your child, over whom you watched so tenderly and for whom you have expressed your highest concept of mother love, and who has grown to manhood and taken advantage of his God-given freedom and the powers that it has been his privilege to unfold and to express as he felt best, he is also God's beloved child. He is ever in the presence of the Father, and the Father is helping him to awaken from the dream of sense and to judge wisely and to discriminate between the worth-while things of Spirit and the false and undesirable things of immaturity.

Trust this dear boy to the Father, dear, and know without doubt that he is being lifted up and set free, and brought into an entirely new consciousness of life and love and power and freedom and success. Even though he should not at present know how to get into and redeem his body and set it in order, he is getting needed lessons and will not have to suffer for the same mistakes again.

\*     \*     \*

We'll help you to know how to speak the Truth to this dear little daughter, to set her free from the limitations that have hindered her progress, and to encourage her in expressing herself through all her senses and powers. She is God's child, and He has created her like Himself, perfect in every part and free to express herself.

Think of your child as God's child, and as God's child ever abiding in His love and surrounded with peace and plenty. This is the truth: Your child *is* God's child. And she does inherit from the divine Father-Mother the perfect Christ Mind.

Something has interfered with the full, free, harmonious development of her faculties. But this is only a temporary condition. And as we who love her think of her in the true light and hold that the Christ Mind is now awakening and quickening and developing all her faculties, she will respond. Her soul does not really want to give way to negation and resentment. But error thoughts have been building up, and she says and does things that her lack of good judgment makes her feel will help her. The Truth spoken with faith and power and love to her soul will break up the old states of mind, and she will begin to take hold for herself.

Assure her daily, as many times as is necessary, that she is perfectly safe and that no one is going to disturb her or take her away. She is at home with those who love her and who know her to be God's child. Talk to her just as though she were expressing herself in a perfectly normal way. That which you think of her and the way in which you appeal to her will determine her reactions.

\*   \*   \*

The love that is the fulfilling of the law is not the personal affection and the clinging to personality that is the usual expression of a happily mated man and woman. Love that fulfills the law is the great sense of unity that prompts the soul to seek the understanding and practice of that which is for the welfare not only of the beloved but of all humanity. When woman recognizes the divine in men and inspires them to express it, she has no difficulty in living happily with a man to whom she has been drawn. When man understands women and adores the divine qualities in them he will be endowed with power from on high to live so that perfect harmony results.

Printed U.S.A.

21-F-8675-5M-8-86